THE BIBLE STORY

VOLUME X

———•—•———

ONWARD TO GLORY

(From the Ascension of Christ to His Coming Kingdom)

PAINTING BY RUSSELL HARLAN © BY REVIEW AND HERALD

Timothy learns the Holy Scriptures.

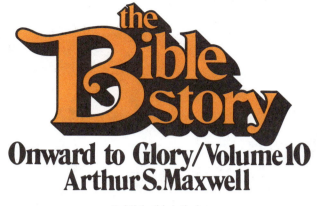

the Bible Story

Onward to Glory/Volume 10
Arthur S. Maxwell

Published jointly by

PACIFIC PRESS® PUBLISHING ASSOCIATION
Nampa, ID 83653
Oshawa, Ontario, Canada

REVIEW AND HERALD PUBLISHING ASSOCIATION
Washington, DC 20039-0555
Hagerstown, MD 21740

CONTENTS

Part I—Stories of the First Christian Church

ACTS 1:12-12:19   PAGE

Part II—Stories of the First Christian Missionaries

ACTS 13:1-28:31

5

Part III—Stories of the First Christian Letters

Part IV—Stories of Christ's Final Triumph

Indexes

PART I

Stories of the First Christian Church

(Acts 1:12-12:19)

STORY 1

The Flame From Heaven

OW HAPPY the angels must have been on that glorious ascension day! I can almost feel their radiant gladness, can't you?

Joyfully they crowd about their beloved Lord as they speed heavenward singing David's victory song:

"Lift up your heads, O ye gates;

And be ye lift up, ye everlasting doors;

And the King of glory shall come in."

"Who is this King of glory?" asks a voice from the dwelling place of God.

Cry the angels in unison,

"The Lord strong and mighty,

The Lord mighty in battle.

Lift up your heads, O ye gates;

Even lift them up, ye everlasting doors;

And the King of glory shall come in."

Jesus is indeed a conqueror. He has battled with Satan

9

After His life of toil and sacrifice Jesus ascended to heaven where He was joyfully received by the angelic hosts, many of whom had attended Him in His last sufferings.

and won. He has died and risen again. He has proved that God's love is stronger than the devil's hate, and that all of Satan's plans must fail.

Now He takes the place long waiting for Him "on the right hand of the Majesty on high." But does He, amid all this glory, forget His humble followers on the earth? No indeed. Instead He watches over them more lovingly than ever, hoping they will not fail Him.

He tells the angels all about them—about Peter, James, John, Thomas, and all the rest—so that they too become deeply interested in His earthly friends. Eagerly they await His call to fly to their help in times of need.

Meanwhile, down on the earth, there is much excitement in a certain room in Jerusalem. It is packed to the doors with a hundred and twenty people. Among them are the eleven disciples, who have just seen Jesus ascend to heaven from the top of the Mount of Olives. The others are full of questions.

"Did you really see Him go up into the sky?" asks one. "How far did He go before you couldn't see Him any more?"

"And about that cloud," asks another. "Was it a real cloud or a cloud of angels?"

"Tell us about the two young men in white," urges somebody else. "Are you sure Jesus sent them? Did they really say Jesus would come back someday?"

They remember how He told them to wait in Jerusalem until they should receive "power from on high." What can this mean? What power? What for? What will it do to them?

THE FLAME FROM HEAVEN

Nobody can answer these questions. They will have to wait and see. But they feel that if Jesus is going to send them power from heaven, they must get ready to receive it. So they begin to pray, and continue in prayer.

They have some wonderful prayer meetings. I can hear them thanking God for sending Jesus from heaven to live among them and die for them. I can hear them, too, thanking Him for the friendship of Jesus, and for all the lovely times they had together with Him.

And I am sure some of them tell God how much they need courage and strength to witness for Jesus, and how they want to be brave and good and true.

As they get closer to God they come closer to one another. Some begin to ask forgiveness for hasty words they have said, or for unkind deeds they have done. There are tears in many eyes as some clasp hands, saying, "Of course, I forgive you; please forgive me!" So they all begin to know something of the joy that comes from keeping that beautiful commandment of Jesus: "That ye love one another, as I have loved you."

Day after day they stay together, waiting for Jesus to keep His promise, waiting for the power from heaven. Then, just seven weeks after the crucifixion, when the day of Pentecost has fully come, something very wonderful happens.

Suddenly there is a sound of a rushing mighty wind. It rattles the windows, slams the doors, shakes the whole house.

Then upon every one of them there appears a tongue of fire. Those at the back of the room see it flaming upon Peter, James, John, and the rest of the apostles; while they, in turn, see it flashing from the humblest disciple present.

For a moment it seems as though the whole house is on fire. And so it is!

Until this moment the room has been hushed and quiet. Only the voices of people praying have been heard. Now, with this rushing mighty wind and these tongues of flame all is changed. In one swift moment everybody is filled with zeal and activity. All begin talking at once about the wonderful love of Jesus.

They feel they have prayed enough; now they must go out and tell the world about their risen Lord.

From this fire-filled room ten dozen men and women go forth, aflame for God, eager to carry the light of His love to the uttermost parts of the earth.

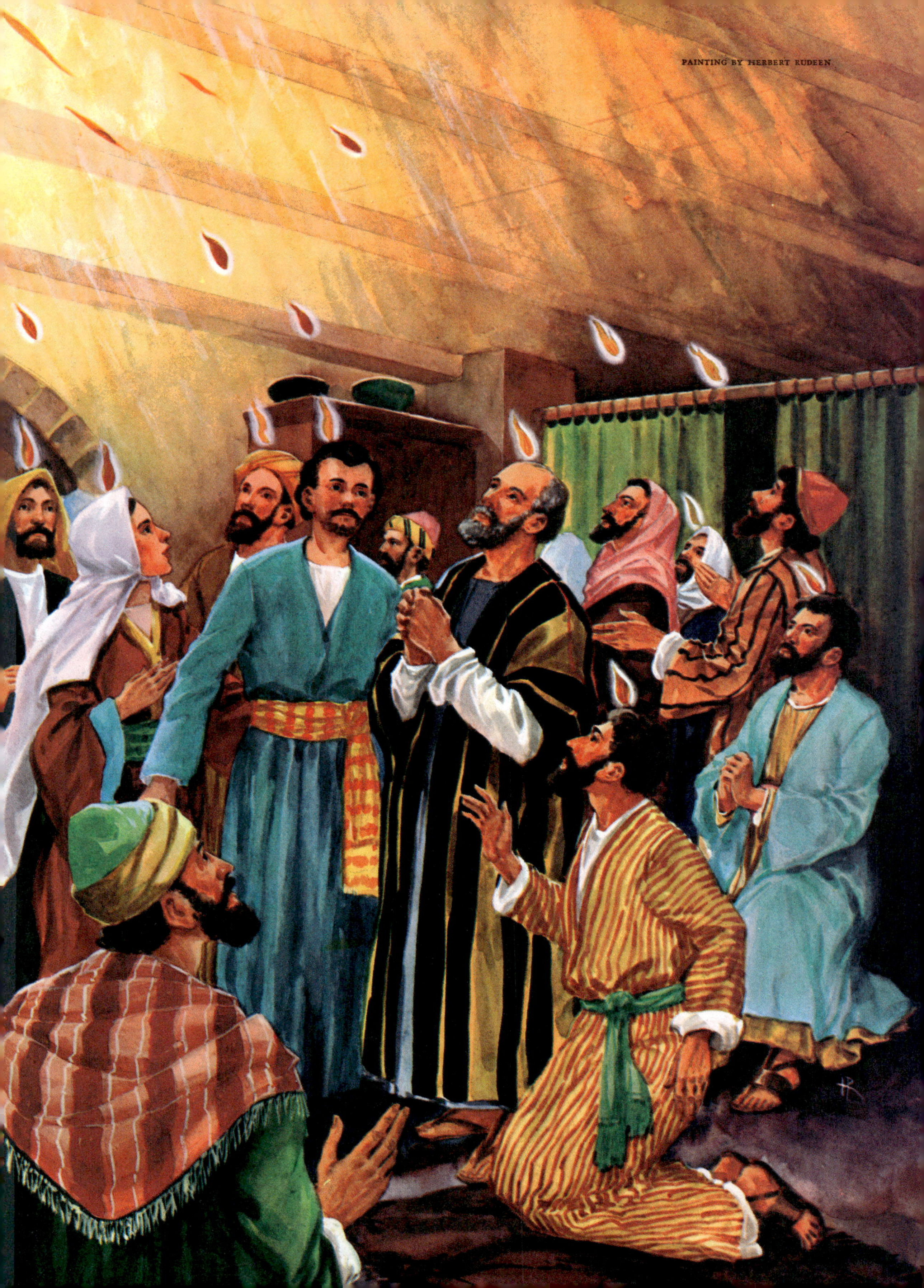

PAINTING BY HERBERT RUDEEN

STORY 2

Men on Fire

TO THE great surprise of the disciples, all the foreign visitors in Jerusalem seem to understand what they say. The faces of strangers from other lands light up as they hear the message of the love of Jesus told them by these humble and unlearned men. "Are not all these who are speaking Galileans?" they ask. "And how is it that we hear, each of us in his own native language?"

It is beyond belief that these men from northern Palestine, who have never been to school, can talk in so many languages—to "Parthians and Medes and Elamites and residents of Mesopotamia, Judea, and Cappadocia, Pontus and Asia, Phrygia and Pamphylia, Egypt and the parts of Libya belonging to Cyrene, and visitors from Rome, . . . Cretans and Arabians."

"How can it be," ask these foreigners, "that we hear them telling in our own tongues the mighty works of God?"

"They must be drunk," says someone. "They are filled with new wine."

MEN ON FIRE

This is too much for Peter. He knows the true answer. The King of glory has remembered His old friends and has sent them the promised power.

Standing where he can be both seen and heard, he cries:

"Men of Judea and all who dwell in Jerusalem, . . . these men are not drunk, as you suppose, since it is only the third hour of the day; but this is what was spoken by the prophet Joel: And in the last days it shall be, God declares, that I will pour out My Spirit upon all flesh, and your sons and your daughters shall prophesy, and your young men shall see visions, and your old men shall dream dreams. . . .

"Men of Israel, hear these words: Jesus of Nazareth, a man attested to you by God with mighty works and wonders and signs which God did through Him in your midst, as you yourselves know—this Jesus . . . you crucified and killed by the hands of lawless men.

"But God raised Him up, having loosed the pangs of death, because it was not possible for Him to be held by it. . . .

"Brethren, I may say to you confidently of the patriarch David that he both died and was buried, and his tomb is with us to this day. Being therefore a prophet . . . he foresaw and spoke of the resurrection of the Christ. . . .

"This Jesus God raised up, and of that we all are witnesses.

"Being therefore exalted at the right hand of God, and having received from the Father the promise of the Holy Spirit, He has poured out this which you see and hear."

What a sermon! With flashing eye and powerful voice Peter tells about Jesus—His life, His death, His resurrection, and the wonderful way He fulfilled the prophecies of old.

Fearing neither priest nor ruler, scribe nor Pharisee, he cries, "Let all the house of Israel therefore know assuredly that God has made Him both Lord and Christ, this Jesus whom you crucified."

Even the disciples are amazed at Peter's boldness. What can have happened to him? How can he hold thousands spellbound like this?

Something *has* happened to him. The power of God has come upon him. His heart has been set on fire by the Holy Spirit. Peter the coward, who thrice denied his Lord, has become Peter the fearless, a mighty witness for Jesus.

Now voices are being raised in the crowd.

"Brethren, what shall we do?" they cry.

"Repent," answers Peter, "and be baptized every one of you in the name of Jesus Christ for the forgiveness of your sins; and you shall receive the gift of the Holy Spirit. For the promise is to you and to your children, and to all that are far off, every one whom the Lord our God calls to Him."

On and on he speaks, pleading with young and old to give their hearts to the Lord. "Save yourselves from this crooked generation!" he cries.

The response is marvelous. Three thousand people accept Jesus. The biggest baptism in history begins—and the Christian church is born.

STORY 3

A Beggar Healed

WITH the coming of the fire of God into their hearts the disciples discovered that they could not only preach but heal! Besides being able to talk in several languages, they could make people well from all sorts of diseases. They had become both preachers and doctors at once.

Now, instead of one person performing miracles, there were a hundred. The work that Jesus did alone was now done by many. No wonder all Jerusalem was stirred!

Going up to the Temple one day, Peter and John saw a lame man being carried by his friends to the gate where he used to sit by the hour, asking passers-by for money.

They had seen him there many times before, and had felt sorry for him. Now they could really help him.

"Look at us," said Peter, to call the lame man's attention.

The beggar looked, expecting a gift, but the apostles had something far better for him than money.

A BEGGAR HEALED

"I have no silver and gold," said Peter, "but I give you what I have; in the name of Jesus Christ of Nazareth, walk."

Taking the lame man by the hand, Peter raised him up. Immediately his feet and ankles became strong. "And leaping up he stood and walked and entered the temple with them, walking and leaping and praising God."

You can imagine what happened next. As the healed man clung to Peter and John in joy and gratitude, "all the people ran together unto them . . . greatly wondering." Pushing and shoving, the crowd pressed forward to see this great sight.

Everybody knew this poor man. They had seen him begging at the Temple gate for years—since he was a boy. For more than forty years he had been lame. Yet here he was walking and leaping about in the most amazing way. What a miracle!

As the people crowded around, Peter saw another opportunity to tell them about Jesus. "Men of Israel," he cried in a voice that could be heard above the hubbub, "why do you wonder at this, or why do you stare at us, as though by our own power or piety we had made him walk?"

Then he went on to tell how it was really Jesus who had done it. "His name, by faith in His name, has made this man strong" and given him "this perfect health in the presence of you all."

Then he pleaded with the people to repent of their sins and give their hearts to Jesus.

As he spoke, more and more people joined the crowd, until almost everybody in the Temple was there. Many of the priests

19

PAINTING BY RUSSELL HARLAN   ©   BY REVIEW AND HERALD

Outside the Beautiful Gate of the Temple a poor beggar who had been lame all his life was healed by Peter, who said, "In the name of Jesus Christ of Nazareth rise up and walk."

came to listen too, and they were anything but pleased—especially when they heard Peter say, "You denied the Holy and Righteous One, and asked for a murderer to be granted to you, and killed the Author of life, whom God raised from the dead."

This was the very thing the priests had feared! The disciples of Jesus were claiming that their leader had been raised from the dead! This must be stopped at once. They called the Temple guard, but Peter went on unafraid.

With deep tenderness he said, "And now, brethren, I know that you acted in ignorance, as did also your rulers. But what God foretold by the mouth of all the prophets, that His Christ should suffer, He thus fulfilled. Repent therefore, and turn again, that your sins may be blotted out, that times of refreshing may come from the presence of the Lord, and that He may send the Christ appointed for you, Jesus, whom heaven must receive until the time for establishing all that God spoke by the mouth of His holy prophets from of old. . . .

"You are the sons of the prophets and of the covenant which God gave to your fathers, saying to Abraham, 'And in your posterity shall all the families of the earth be blessed.' God, having raised up His servant, sent Him to you first, to bless you in turning every one of you from your wickedness."

At this moment the captain of the Temple forced his way through the crowd and arrested both Peter and John and led them away to prison. But he was too late. The people had heard the message. As they went to their homes that night many more decided that Jesus of Nazareth was indeed the Christ, the Saviour of the world.

STORY 4

From Prison to Pulpit

NEXT morning there was a big meeting of the Temple leaders. Annas and Caiaphas were there, the very ones who had presided at the trial of Jesus. Presently Peter and John were called before them.

"By what power, or by what name, did you do this?" asked the high priest.

Without a trace of fear Peter replied, "By the name of Jesus Christ of Nazareth, whom you crucified, whom God raised from the dead, by Him this man is standing before you well."

"And there is salvation in no one else," he added, "for there is no other name under heaven given among men by which we must be saved."

So Peter told his story once more, speaking so boldly that the priests and rulers were astonished. They couldn't understand how a poor, uneducated fisherman could talk like this. As for the miracle that had been wrought, they couldn't say

21

a thing. Not only was the man who had been healed known to every one of them, but here he was in their midst, standing near the two apostles, ready to speak up for them if need be.

"What shall we do with these men?" the priests asked of one another when the council room had been cleared. "For that a notable sign has been performed through them is manifest to all the inhabitants of Jerusalem, and we cannot deny it."

Finally they decided that they would tell the apostles that they must not preach about Jesus any more, and then let them go. But they did not realize the kind of men these fishermen had become.

Called back into court, and hearing the decision of the priests and rulers, "Peter and John answered and said unto them, 'Whether it is right in the sight of God to listen to you rather than to God, you must judge. For we cannot but speak of what we have seen and heard.'"

"You had better not!" said the high priest. But the apostles went away with no thought of stopping their work. Later, in their upper room they had a wonderful time together, thanking God for the way He had helped them and praying for strength to witness yet more boldly in the future.

FROM PRISON TO PULPIT

"Now, Lord," prayed one of them, "behold their threatenings: and grant unto Thy servants, that with all boldness they may speak Thy word, by stretching forth Thine hand to heal; and that signs and wonders may be done by the name of Thy holy child Jesus."

The prayer was answered. More power came from heaven. More people were healed. More great sermons were preached. Indeed, "with great power gave the apostles witness of the resurrection of the Lord Jesus: and great grace was upon them all."

"By the hands of the apostles were many signs and wonders wrought among the people. . . . Insomuch that they brought forth the sick into the streets, and laid them on beds and couches, that at the least the shadow of Peter passing by might overshadow some of them."

It was just like the days when Jesus had been there! People began flocking into Jerusalem from nearby villages, "bringing sick folks, and them which were vexed with unclean spirits: and they were healed every one."

This was too much for the priests and rulers. They became very angry. They could not bear to see these followers of Jesus more popular than themselves. So once more they had them arrested and put in the common prison.

But these men couldn't be imprisoned. No sooner were they in than they were out again.

"The angel of the Lord by night opened the prison doors, and brought them forth, and said, Go, stand and speak in the temple to the people all the words of this life."

So Peter and John went straight from the prison to the pulpit, as it were. And there in the Temple they went on witnessing for Jesus just as though nothing had happened.

The best of it was that the priests knew nothing about the apostles' escape. They made ready for their trial and "sent to the prison to have them brought." But there were no prisoners there. In a great fluster the officers returned, saying, "We found the prison securely locked and the sentries standing at the doors, but when we had opened it we found no one inside."

You can imagine the feelings of everyone in that council room. "What!" cried all. "The prisoners gone? Where can they be? How did they escape through locked doors?"

24

FROM PRISON TO PULPIT

Suddenly a messenger came rushing in with the astounding news that the escaped prisoners were actually "standing in the temple, and teaching the people."

"Bring them here!" cried the chief priest, and the guard went in search of them.

They were soon back, this time with Peter and several others.

"We strictly charged you not to teach in this name," said the high priest hotly, "yet here you have filled Jerusalem with your teaching and you intend to bring this man's blood on us."

"We must obey God rather than men," said Peter, which made the priests and rulers more angry still.

Just then Gamaliel stood up. He was a member of the council and "held in honor by all the people."

"Take care what you do with these men," he warned. "If this plan or this undertaking is of men, it will fail; but if it is of God, you will not be able to overthrow them."

These were wise words, and the council heeded them. It was decided to let the apostles off with a beating.

The lashes hurt, but when the beating was over, the apostles left the council "rejoicing that they were counted worthy to suffer shame for His name. And daily in the temple, and in every house, they ceased not to teach and preach Jesus Christ."

STORY 5

Sons of Encouragement

I T SEEMS hard to believe, but within a few months of the crucifixion of Jesus five thousand men had accepted Him as their Saviour and been baptized in His name.

These men, with their women and children, must have been quite a sizable part of the population of Jerusalem at that time. No wonder the priests and rulers were upset!

As for the new believers, they were full of love for their Lord and for one another. The Bible says that they "were of one heart and soul, and no one said that any of the things which he possessed was his own, but they had everything in common. . . . There was not a needy person among them, for as many as were possessors of lands or houses sold them, and brought the proceeds of what was sold and laid it at the apostles' feet." The money was then given away to the believers according to their need.

One of those who sold a field and brought the money to the apostles was a man called Joseph, a native of Cyprus. He

26

gave his gift so gladly, so graciously, that everybody was cheered. Indeed, Peter and John and the others were so happy about it that they gave him the nickname Barnabas, which means "son of encouragement."

What a lovely name! Wouldn't you like somebody to call you that someday? Maybe Mother or Dad? You know how to make this happen? Just try being like Joseph of Cyprus. Do all you are asked to do with a happy, cheerful spirit.

Sons of encouragement (and daughters of encouragement too) are welcome everywhere. They are wanted at home, at school, and in church. Parents, teachers, preachers, and businessmen are always looking for them.

Not all the people, however, were so nice about helping the early church as Barnabas was. Some brought their money grudgingly. Some thought the apostles were asking too much. Others said this pooling of the money wasn't a good idea at all.

Among these were a man named Ananias and his wife Sapphira.

They had heard the message about the wonderful Teacher of Nazareth who had risen from the dead. They loved His teachings, and believed He must be the Messiah of Israel. And when they saw many of the new disciples selling their property and giving the money to the apostles to feed the poor and help the work, they felt that they should do the same.

So they dedicated a piece of land to God and sold it. The Bible doesn't say how much they got for it, but it was probably a very good price and more than they had expected.

When the money was in their hands they counted it several times. Soon they began to feel that it was really too much to give just then. Maybe they should keep some for themselves. After all, there was that comfortable couch Ananias wanted, and that beautiful new dress Sapphira had set her heart on.

They talked it over together and decided to give a part—a nice large part—to God and keep the rest. Who would know? And couldn't they do what they liked with their own money?

Putting the coins in a bag, Ananias set out for the place where Peter was receiving the people's gifts. He felt sure that the apostle would praise him warmly for giving so much.

But when he got there he found he couldn't look Peter in

the eye. Indeed, he felt a great urge to put the moneybag on the table and run.

Something bothered him. Peter seemed to be looking clear through him, reading his thoughts. He was.

"Ananias," he said, without a word of thanks for the money he had brought, "why has Satan filled your heart to lie to the Holy Spirit and to keep back part of the proceeds of the land? While it remained unsold, did it not remain your own? And after it was sold, was it not at your disposal? How is it that you have contrived this deed in your heart? You have not lied to men but to God."

So Peter knew what he and his wife had planned in the privacy of their own home! How could he have found out?

The shock was too much for Ananias. There and then he "fell down and died." Some young men carried out his body and buried it.

Meanwhile Sapphira was waiting for him to return. What could be keeping him? she wondered. After a while she began to get worried. How could he have taken so long to go so short a distance? Of course, the apostles might have given him some special honor for making so large a donation.

After waiting three hours she thought it was time to go and look for him.

Peter was still standing at the table, receiving gifts from believers when she entered. Before she could say anything he surprised her by asking, "Tell me whether you sold the land for so much," mentioning the amount of money Ananias had handed in.

"Yes, for so much," she said, without a blush.

"How is it that you have agreed together to tempt the Spirit of the Lord?" asked Peter.

Before she could answer he added, "Hark! the feet of those that have buried your husband are at the door, and they will carry you out."

"My husband buried!" I can almost hear her crying. "Ananias dead!"

A moment later she too collapsed and died, and the young men "carried her out and buried her beside her husband."

"And great fear came upon the whole church." No wonder! They could see that the Holy Spirit, by whom such mighty miracles had been wrought, was not a power to be played with—or lied to.

They saw too the great difference between Barnabas, the son of encouragement, and Ananias, the son of discouragement. One brought cheer, the other fear. One, by his gracious generosity, blessed the church with happiness. The other, by his selfishness, plunged it into sorrow. We must decide which kind of person we want to be.

STORY 6

Man With the Shining Face

T HE DEATH of Ananias and Sapphira struck the first sad note in the story of the early church. But it was not the last. Many more followed, one after another.

First, came grumbling. One group of believers thought it was not getting as much money from the general fund as another group. These people said their widows were overlooked while others were given plenty.

I am sure Peter never meant to favor one group above another. He just had too many things to do. Like Moses, he was trying to be a preacher and a teacher, a judge and a businessman, all at the same time, and nobody, not even an apostle, could do so many jobs properly.

Then, too, the number of believers was growing every day. The Bible says that they "multiplied greatly in Jerusalem, and a great many of the priests were obedient to the faith."

It must have been thrilling to see so many people, even priests, joining the church, but caring for them all soon be-

31

came such a big task that the apostles had no time to preach.

There were twelve of them again now, for a man called Matthias had been chosen to take the place of Judas. But even so, they couldn't possibly look after the needs of so large a congregation and keep on with their preaching at the same time.

So they called a meeting and said to the believers, "It is not right that we should give up preaching the word of God to serve tables. Therefore, brethren, pick out from among you seven men of good repute, full of the Spirit and of wisdom, whom we may appoint to this duty. But we will devote ourselves to prayer and to the ministry of the word."

The believers were pleased at this suggestion and chose Stephen, "a man full of faith and of the Holy Spirit," and Philip, Prochorus, Nicanor, Timon, Parmenas, and Nicolas.

When the election was over, the apostles "prayed and laid their hands upon them." These seven men were the first deacons of the Christian church.

Stephen, the head deacon, was a remarkable man. He might well have been an apostle if Jesus had met him in Galilee. "Full of grace and power," he "did great wonders and signs among the people." He was a great speaker, too, and got into many a debate with people who said that Christ was not the Messiah. And "they could not withstand the wisdom and the spirit with which he spoke."

For a while he took the spotlight from Peter, James, John, and the rest of the apostles. What a deacon he was!

So powerful a preacher was he that the elders and scribes, thinking he must be the ringleader of the followers of

Christ, had him arrested and brought before the Sanhedrin.

The charge against him was that he never ceased "to speak words against this holy place and the law" and that he had said, "Jesus of Nazareth will destroy this place, and will change the customs which Moses delivered to us."

It wasn't true, of course. They were just twisting words, as they had done when Christ was in that selfsame place.

As for Stephen, he stood there calmly, without a trace of fear, his heart at peace with God.

"And gazing at him, all who sat in the council saw that his face was like the face of an angel."

I doubt that any of those councilors had ever seen an angel, but somehow Stephen's face, all aglow with trust and confidence in his beloved Lord and Saviour, was so radiantly beautiful that it made them think of angels.

When the high priest asked him whether the charges made against him were true, Stephen defended himself with great power. Showing a marvelous grasp of the Holy Scriptures, he reminded the council how God had led His people from the days of Abraham until that very moment. He talked of Moses and the deliverance from Egypt and of Solomon and the building of the Temple. But when he reminded them that "the Most High does not dwell in houses made with hands" they began to get restless. So he unburdened his heart and told them the straight truth he felt they should hear.

"You stiff-necked people," he said, "uncircumcised in heart and ears, you always resist the Holy Spirit. As your fathers did, so do you. Which of the prophets did not your fathers persecute? And they killed those who announced beforehand the coming of the Righteous One, whom you have now betrayed and murdered, you who received the law as delivered by angels and did not keep it."

The members of the council ground their teeth in anger.

Suddenly, looking up, Stephen cried aloud, "Behold, I see the heavens opened, and the Son of man standing at the right hand of God."

"Blasphemy!" shrieked the councilors. Then, stopping their ears, they rushed upon him and "cast him out of the city and stoned him."

As the hail of stones, flung by those cruel and angry men, began to strike him, Stephen fell on his knees and prayed, saying, "Lord Jesus, receive my spirit. . . . Lord, do not hold this sin against them."

"And when he had said this, he fell asleep."

So died the man with the shining face. He was the first martyr of the Christian church.

STORY 7

Seeds in the Wind

THE STONING of Stephen was a great shock to the thousands of believers in Jerusalem.

Everything had gone so well that nobody had dreamed anything like this would happen. But now word spread that the Sanhedrin was planning to stamp out the new sect before it should get any stronger. One councilor, a man named Saul of Tarsus, was already going from house to house arresting men and women suspected of being followers of Jesus and putting them in prison.

Those were sad days, and saddest of all for the children whose fathers and mothers were taken away to jail.

The Bible says that "there was a great persecution against the church which was at Jerusalem; and they were all scattered abroad throughout the regions of Judaea and Samaria, except the apostles."

Hundreds of Christians fled from the city. Whole families left as quickly as they could. Some went north toward Syria,

35

others south to Egypt. Some took ship from Caesarea for Cyprus, while others may have traveled as far as Italy, Spain, and even England.

As the priests and rulers saw them go, no doubt they said to one another, "This is the last we shall hear of all this nonsense about Jesus of Nazareth." But they were mistaken. For "they that were scattered abroad went every where preaching the word." Like seeds blown by a strong wind, the followers of Jesus went ever farther and farther afield, finally settling down and taking root in a thousand towns and villages of the Roman Empire.

It had not been long since the priests and rulers had thought to finish with Jesus by nailing Him to a cross, only to learn later that He had risen from the dead. Now, as they sought to crush the work He had begun in the hearts and lives of men, they saw it growing and spreading everywhere. The more they tried to kill it, the bigger and stronger it became.

One of those who left Jerusalem at this time was Philip, the second of the seven deacons. He went to Samaria and began to preach Christ to the people there. In the power of the Holy Spirit he performed miracles of healing as the Master Himself had done.

The response was marvelous. A messenger was sent to Jerusalem for help. Peter and John went at once to see what God had wrought. They prayed with the new believers, and the Holy Spirit was poured out upon them.

QUADE

It must have been hard for some of the Jews to believe that this could happen in Samaria, but it did, right before their eyes, and it was clear proof that Jews and Samaritans could become one in Christ.

The most important convert in Samaria was a man called Simon. He was a magician, and he had had a lot of influence in the city. But now he was nobody, for Philip, Peter, and John worked far greater miracles than he had ever performed.

How he craved the same power they had! He even offered to buy it!

"Your silver perish with you," Peter said to him, "because you thought you could obtain the gift of God with money! You have neither part nor lot in this matter, for your heart is not right before God. Repent therefore of this wickedness of yours, and pray to the Lord that, if possible, the intent of your heart may be forgiven you. For I see that you are in the gall of bitterness and in the bond of iniquity."

Simon was repentant. He hadn't understood that there are some things money cannot buy.

"Pray for me," he said, "that nothing of what you have said may come upon me."

STORY 8

An Old Book Glows

P HILIP was still in Samaria when God sent him on another errand.

"Rise and go toward the south to the road that goes down from Jerusalem to Gaza," said the heavenly messenger.

That was all. Just go! So he went.

As he walked along the road he must have wondered why God wanted him to go to Gaza. Could it be that he was to preach the same message there as he had in Samaria? Or had God something else in mind?

By and by he heard the familiar cloppety-clop, cloppety-clop, of horses' hoofs and the squeaking of wooden wheels and axles.

Looking up, he saw a well-dressed Ethiopian going by in a fine chariot and recognized him as one of the chief officials of Candace, queen of Ethiopia, and the treasurer of that country. The man had been to Jerusalem to worship God in the Temple and was returning home by the desert road.

Suddenly a voice said to Philip, "Go up and join this chariot."

Philip ran, no doubt wondering what to say to this well-to-do stranger.

Seeing Philip running toward him, the Ethiopian told his servant to rein in the horses. As the chariot stopped, Philip noticed that the man was reading from a scroll containing the book of Isaiah. So he asked, "Do you understand what you are reading?"

It was a strange question to ask of a man he had never met before, but the Ethiopian was not offended. Instead, he invited Philip to get into his chariot and began to ask questions about the text which says that God's Servant will be "led as a sheep to the slaughter."

"About whom, pray, does the prophet say this?" asked the Ethiopian. "About himself or about someone else?"

Philip couldn't have wished for a better chance to talk about Jesus. Now he knew why God had told him to walk along the Gaza road! Of course! God had known that this honest seeker after truth would be traveling this way. How fortunate that Philip had obeyed the call!

And now, "beginning with this scripture he told him the good news of Jesus."

What a Bible study that must have been!

In a way it was just the same Bible study that Jesus had given Cleopas and his friend on the way to Emmaus. Only now it was given by Philip to an Ethiopian on the way to Gaza.

True, Jesus began with Moses, and Philip began with Isaiah. But that didn't matter. They both came to the same conclusion.

I am sure there wasn't a prophecy about Jesus in all the Old Testament that Philip left out, nor a question about Him that the Ethiopian didn't ask.

As the two men journeyed together, the precious old Book they held in their hands glowed with the glory of God. Both felt that the King of glory was speaking directly to them.

And can't you hear Philip saying to the Ethiopian as this wonderful Bible study drew to a close, "Won't you accept Jesus as *your* Lord and Saviour? Won't you give your heart to Him now?"

"Yes," said the Ethiopian, "I will indeed."

At that moment they happened to pass a pool of water.

"See, here is water!" said the Ethiopian. "What is to prevent my being baptized?"

"Nothing," said Philip.

So the Ethiopian "commanded the chariot to stop, and they both went down into the water." And Philip baptized him then and there.

When they came up out of the water Philip disappeared, being caught away by the Spirit of the Lord.

As for the Ethiopian, he "went on his way rejoicing," to tell the wonderful story of Jesus to his queen and countrymen.

STORY 9

Enemy Becomes a Champion

OF ALL the enemies of the early Christians the worst was Saul. As a Pharisee, he hated the followers of Jesus. The Bible tells us that he "made havock of the church."

Having done his worst in Jerusalem, he decided to follow those who had left the city and were preaching about Jesus in other parts of the country.

"And Saul, still breathing threats and murder against the disciples of the Lord, went to the high priest, and asked him for letters to the synagogues at Damascus, so that if he found any belonging to the Way, men or women, he might bring them bound to Jerusalem."

With his mind full of plans for wiping out the Christians in short order, he starts on his journey, leading a company of men who are to help him in his wicked work. For several days they travel northward over the rough, winding roads.

They are almost at Damascus, within sight of the city,

when a wonderful thing happens. It is midday. Everybody is hot, tired, and thirsty. Suddenly a light "above the brightness of the sun" shines about them. The whole party is struck down. The caravan comes to a dead stop.

Blinded by the dazzling light and unable to rise, Saul hears a voice calling to him, "Saul, Saul, why do you persecute Me?"

"Who are You, Lord?" he asks.

"I am Jesus, whom you are persecuting."

Saul is astounded. How can Jesus be here on the Damascus road? Can this be the very person who the Christians declare has risen from the dead? Is He indeed the King of glory as they claim? If so, what a dreadful mistake he has made in treating His followers so cruelly!

A few moments before, Saul was a proud, self-important man; now he is humble; he sees how foolish he has been.

"What shall I do, Lord?" he asks.

"Rise, and enter the city," says Jesus, "and you will be told what you are to do."

At this Saul staggers to his feet, while his friends, still trembling with fright, crowd around, offering to help him. But there is nothing they can do save lead him by the hand. He is blind.

So Saul arrives in Damascus. Not as he had planned, striding proudly at the head of a group of men sworn to stamp out the Christian faith; but stumbling forward, humble and penitent, to learn the will of Jesus and serve Him faithfully forever.

In the city at last, Saul goes to stay with a man called Judas, and there, for three days, he neither eats nor drinks. Shocked by what happened to him on the Damascus road,

44

and sorry for all his mistakes, he wants only to pray. And here on his knees he asks Jesus to forgive him and show him what to do next.

About this time Jesus appears to Ananias, one of His disciples in Damascus, and says, "Rise, and go to the street called Straight, and inquire in the house of Judas for a man of Tarsus named Saul; for, behold, he is praying."

Ananias is alarmed. The last person he wants to meet is Saul of Tarsus. He knows him well, and all his cruel deeds. "Lord, I have heard by many of this man," he says, "how much evil he has done to Thy saints at Jerusalem."

But Jesus replies, "Go, for he is a chosen instrument of Mine to carry My name before the Gentiles and kings and the sons of Israel."

Ananias obeys. He finds Saul in the home of Judas, praying, as Jesus had said. There, putting his hands on him, he says, "Brother Saul, the Lord Jesus who appeared to you on the road by which you came, has sent me that you may regain your sight and be filled with the Holy Spirit."

At once Saul's eyes are opened. He can see again. And the first person he looks upon is a disciple of Jesus, who baptizes him into the church.

That was a very lovely thing that Ananias said—"Brother Saul." It is hard to call someone brother who has been unkind to you. To Saul's ears it must have sounded very beautiful indeed. It may have helped more than we know in leading him to make his decision for Christ.

His sight restored, and a baptized member of the church, Saul begins to witness for his Lord. "Straightway" he preaches Christ in the synagogues, "that He is the Son of God."

Some of the disciples refuse to have anything to do with him, remembering how he persecuted the Christians in Jerusalem. But he insists that he now loves Jesus as much as they do.

As for the Jews who had expected him to stamp out the Christian faith in Damascus, they are at first amazed, then angry. They plan to take Saul's life, but news of the plot is brought to Saul, and while the Jews watch the city gates night and day to kill him, some of the disciples put him in a basket, and in the dead of night let him down over the wall.

Thus Saul of Tarsus escapes from Damascus to become Paul the apostle to the Gentiles, one of the greatest champions Jesus has ever had.

≋≋≋≋

STORY 10

The Antelope Lady

≋≋≋≋≋≋≋≋≋≋≋≋≋≋≋≋≋≋

FANCY calling a lady an antelope! But that is what they did. And that is what she was.

Her real name was Tabitha, but the people of Joppa gave her the nickname Dorcas, meaning "gazelle," or "antelope." And I know why. It was because she was always running as quickly as she could from one needy person to another.

But not only are antelopes swift-footed; they are gentle and friendly creatures too, and so was Tabitha. Perhaps she had big bright eyes as they do—eyes that showed interest in people and tender sympathy for them in their trials and sorrows.

This wonderful lady was the life of the Joppa church. She was always thinking up new ways of showing kindness to others. The Bible says that she was "full of good works and acts of charity." When she didn't have her hands full nursing somebody's sick child or talking to some blind person or taking flowers to a shut-in, she made garments of all sorts for the poor.

47

Yet, busy as she was, ever rushing from one thing to another, she was always patient and sweet-tempered, radiating courage and good cheer everywhere she went.

No wonder everybody loved her! No wonder, too, the whole church was plunged into sorrow when she suddenly was taken ill and died.

How did she die? I don't know. Probably because she was worn out helping others. Maybe she caught a germ from some sick person for whom she was caring.

It was the custom in those days to bury a dead person right away, but the people of Joppa couldn't bear to part with their beloved little antelope lady. So they put her body in an upper room and waited.

THE ANTELOPE LADY

Somebody said, "If only Peter were here!"

And somebody else said, "But he is!"

"Where?" asked everybody at once.

"At Lydda, just a few miles away. Only a day or two ago he healed a man named Aeneas who had been sick in bed for eight years."

"Let's send for him then!" cried all, and two men set out for Lydda. Finding Peter, they told him the story of Tabitha and begged him to come at once. He agreed, and the three hurried back to Joppa as fast as they could.

Coming into the room where the body of Dorcas was lying, Peter found it full of weeping widows whom Dorcas

had helped during her lifetime. They showed Peter coats and other garments she had made for them.

Gently he asked them all to leave. Then he knelt beside the bed and prayed.

What a picture! The big fisherman of Galilee on his knees before God asking Him to give life to a dead woman! How earnestly he must have prayed, just as Elisha prayed for the dead son of the "great woman" of Shunem, long, long before.

I can almost hear him saying, "Dear Lord, if it be Thy will, restore this dear woman to life. Thy church in Joppa needs her. Dorcas, they call her, Lord, and such she has been —a gazelle, an antelope, leaping from one good work to another for the sake of Thy needy ones. Make it possible for her to continue her ministry of love for the glory of Thy name."

THE ANTELOPE LADY

As he rose from his knees he turned to the body and said, "Tabitha, rise." "And she opened her eyes, and when she saw Peter she sat up."

I am sure she did. The last person she expected to see in her room was the famous apostle of whom she had heard so many wonderful stories.

And then, of all things, Peter held out his hand to help her up. I am sure she never forgot that simple kindness as long as she lived. And the smile of joy and thankfulness on his noble, friendly face, stayed with her forever.

Now, calling the saints and widows who had been waiting impatiently outside, Peter "presented her alive."

They could hardly believe their eyes, and their happiness knew no bounds. Their dear, kind antelope lady was back with them again!

As for Dorcas, I am sure she didn't stay around very long. In no time at all she went hurrying off to help somebody else in need.

STORY 11

Animals in the Sky

AFTER bringing Tabitha back to life, Peter stayed on in Joppa for many days in the home of Simon, a tanner. And here it was that he had a very strange vision.

It happened one day at noon while he was waiting for lunch. He had gone up on the flat roof of the house to spend a little while in prayer.

He liked this place, not only because from here he could see the sea that he loved so dearly, but because on the housetop there was nothing between him and heaven, where Jesus his Lord and Saviour was sitting at the right hand of God.

Presently, as he looked up into the sky, he thought he saw something strange coming down. It was like a great sheet, "let down by four corners upon the earth."

As it came nearer and nearer he saw that the sheet was full of all kinds of animals, reptiles, and birds.

Then a voice said to him, "Rise, Peter; kill and eat."

Peter was hungry. The Bible says so. But he was not

52

PAINTING BY WM. HUTCHINSON © BY REVIEW AND HERALD →

In his vision Peter saw a great sheet let down from heaven full of all kinds of birds and animals. By this means God taught him that he should call no man common or unclean.

hungry enough for this. The animals were all unclean according to the laws of Moses.

"No, Lord," he said, "for I have never eaten anything that is common or unclean."

Then the voice spoke again, saying, "What God has cleansed, you must not call common."

This happened three times. Then the sheet and the animals went up into the sky again and disappeared.

Peter was greatly troubled by what he had seen. He felt sure he had been given this vision for some purpose, but what was it? Did God want him to eat unclean food? Surely not. There must be some other explanation.

While he was still thinking about all those animals in the sky he heard a loud knocking on the gate of the house. Then someone called in a loud voice, "Does Simon Peter live here?"

Peter went to the gate and found three men outside.

"What do you want?" he asked.

They told him that they had come all the way from Caesarea to see him, having been sent by Cornelius, a famous Roman centurion.

"Cornelius," they said, "an upright and God-fearing man, . . . was directed by a holy angel to send for you to come to his house, and to hear what you have to say."

Peter's surprise must have shown on his face. A centurion wanting to see him! What about?

He invited the men to come in and stay for the night. In the morning he went off with them to Caesarea.

When they reached the centurion's house he found it crowded with people waiting to see him. He was given a warm welcome, and Cornelius fell on his knees to worship him, as though he were a god.

"Stand up!" said Peter. "I too am a man."

By this time he was beginning to understand the meaning of his vision. To the whole group he said, "You yourselves know how unlawful it is for a Jew to associate with or to visit any one of another nation; but God has shown me that I should not call any man common or unclean. So when I was sent for, I came without objection. I ask then why you sent for me."

Eagerly Cornelius explained. About four days before, he said, at three o'clock in the afternoon, as he was praying, a man in shining clothes had suddenly appeared before him. This beautiful being had told him to send at once to Joppa and find a man called Simon Peter, who was living "in the house of Simon, a tanner, by the seaside."

"The man in shining clothes seemed to know exactly where you lived," said Cornelius, "so I sent to you at once, and you have been kind enough to come. Now therefore we are all here present in the sight of God, to hear all that you have been commanded by the Lord."

This was a great lesson to Peter. Up to this moment he had thought that the kingdom of God was only for Jews. Now he saw how wrong and foolish this idea was. "I perceive that God shows no partiality," he said, "but in every nation any one who fears Him and does what is right is acceptable to Him."

Then he began to talk about Jesus and how He "went about doing good and healing all that were oppressed by the devil."

"I was there," he said. "I was with Him all the time from

the early days in Galilee until He was crucified. I saw Him after He rose from the dead. We ate and drank together."

It was just a simple, personal testimony, but Cornelius and the rest of the people in the room listened spellbound.

"Jesus told us to preach to the people," Peter went on, "and to testify that He is the one ordained by God to be the judge of the living and the dead. To Him all the prophets bear witness that every one who believes in Him receives forgiveness of sins through His name."

Hour after hour he talked, and everybody was carried away by his words. They accepted Jesus as their Saviour without question.

Then something wonderful happened. Even while Peter was speaking, the Holy Spirit "fell on all who heard the word," and they began to praise and glorify God.

Some Jews who were present were shocked. They couldn't understand how God could pour out His Spirit upon Gentiles. But Peter did. Those animals in the sky had told him.

"Can anyone," he asked, "refuse baptism to these people who have received the Holy Spirit just as we have?"

Of course nobody could. And nobody did. God had spoken. These godly Gentiles were just as dear to Him as any of the children of Abraham.

So they were all baptized then and there, and a Roman centurion became a member of the Christian church.

STORY 12

Dungeon Doors Open

B Y THIS time the little company of fire-filled men who had hurried out of the meeting place on the day of Pentecost had become a host of believers. After the conversion of Saul persecution stopped for a while and thousands all over Palestine accepted the gospel. The Bible says that "a great number believed, and turned to the Lord."

But the good times did not last long.

King Herod arrested James, the brother of John, and put him to death. Because he saw this pleased the Jewish leaders, he put Peter in prison, intending to kill him after the Passover.

Having been told that Peter had escaped from prison once before, Herod gave orders that four squads of soldiers should guard him day and night. He wouldn't get out this time!

Meanwhile, the disciples in Jerusalem, having seen James executed, were greatly worried about their beloved Peter. Would he suffer the same dreadful fate?

From early morning till late at night, yes, and all through

the night, they prayed for him. "O Jesus, please save Peter," they cried. "Don't let them kill our dear Peter!"

Day after day, night after night, Peter remained in the prison, while the church pleaded for his release. But nothing happened. The last night came, the night before he was to die. The next morning would see him executed. Would God deliver him?

Chained in his dungeon, Peter thinks back over his past life, how he first met Jesus in Galilee, how he followed Him for more than three years and then, in the last crisis, denied Him. He remembers how he said angrily, "I know not the man!" and then how the cock crowed. Has Jesus forgiven him for that? Will He come and save him now?

It seems impossible. What can anyone do at this late hour? Look at these chains on his hands and feet, the two soldiers in his cell, the locked door, the soldiers outside, the great iron gate at the entrance to the prison. What hope of escape is there? Who could possibly rescue him from such a place?

58

DUNGEON DOORS OPEN

He is dozing, half asleep, when suddenly he feels a blow on his side. He rouses, wondering who struck him, and why.

Now a hand is grasping his and pulling him to his feet.

"Get up quickly!" whispers a voice.

Mysteriously his chains drop off, clanking loudly on the stone floor.

"Dress yourself and put on your sandals," says the stranger.

Peter obeys, dressing as quickly as he can. Then the stranger speaks again.

"Wrap your mantle around you and follow me," he says.

Silently the stranger opens the cell door and passes through it, Peter following, wondering whether he is dreaming.

Past the first guard they go, past the second, then into the courtyard. All is still, save for the dull snoring of the soldiers who seem to be dead asleep.

Ahead looms the great iron gate, beyond which is the city, and freedom. Can they get through? Does this stranger have the key?

As they approach the gate, to Peter's amazement it opens as it were of its own accord.

Through the gate they go, down to the end of the street. Peter turns to thank the stranger who has rescued him, but there is no one there. "Now I am sure," he says to himself, "that the Lord has sent His angel and rescued me from the hand of Herod and from all that the Jewish people were expecting."

Left to himself, Peter, thankful for his cloak so that he can hide his face from any chance passer-by, hurries through the darkened city to the house of Mary, the mother of John Mark, where many disciples are gathered in prayer for him.

He knocks on the door, and, to make sure that the people inside will not be afraid to open it, he calls out his name.

A girl named Rhoda comes to open the door and recognizes Peter's voice. However—just like a girl—she is so happy to think Peter is there that she forgets to let him in, and runs back into the room where the prayer meeting is still going on.

"Peter's here—outside the door!" she cries. "I heard his voice."

"You're mad!" they say to her.

"But I heard him!" she says. "I know it is Peter."

Still they refuse to believe.

Meanwhile, Peter is getting impatient,

afraid that he may be discovered out there on the street. He goes on knocking.

At last they all go to the door and open it. And there he stands. They can hardly believe their eyes.

"Peter!" they cry. "Is it really you?" and they give him such a welcome that he has to beg them to be quiet, lest the soldiers come and find him there. Then he tells them the wonderful story of how an angel rescued him from the prison.

By morning all Jerusalem has heard the exciting news. From one to another the word spreads like wildfire, "Peter has escaped again!" Tongues wag and people chuckle from one end of the city to the other.

Down at the prison there is "no small stir" over the missing prisoner. No wonder, with all those soldiers supposed to be guarding him! But nobody saw anything. Nobody heard anything. He just disappeared.

Herod is furious, but what can he do but call off the execution? There's no one to execute!

As for Peter, a great thankfulness fills his heart. Once more His beloved Jesus has rescued him.

With new courage and hope he goes forth to do an even greater work for the King of glory he adores.

PART II

Stories of the First Christian Missionaries

(Acts 13:1-28:31)

STORY 1

Saul Becomes Paul

A S TROUBLE grew worse in Jerusalem, more and more people who believed in Jesus moved away to other cities. Many went to Antioch in Syria, about three hundred miles to the north. Here they found a warm welcome.

In no time at all they were telling their new friends all about the beloved Carpenter of Nazareth. As a result "a great number believed, and turned unto the Lord."

When this wonderful news reached the apostles they asked Barnabas to go to Antioch and find out what was going on. His friendly nature made him just the right person to send on such a mission. What he found made him very happy, and he so cheered the new believers that many more were "added unto the Lord."

About this time Barnabas became worried about Saul, who had disappeared. A true "son of encouragement," he traveled as far as Tarsus—about a hundred miles west—in search of him. When he found him he asked him to come and

10-5

At Antioch, where the disciples were first called Christians, Saul and Barnabas and Mark were ordained as missionaries to carry the gospel to Cyprus and lands across the sea.

help strengthen the new church he had raised up in Antioch.

Saul agreed. And so began the wonderful partnership of these two good men, which brought so much blessing to so many.

Those must have been great days in Antioch. The Bible says that the disciples were first called Christians there. No doubt the kindly spirit of Barnabas and the forceful preaching of Saul had much to do with it. Both of them so uplifted Christ that people wanted to belong to Him and to be known as His followers.

One day the presence of God was felt in the church in a very special way. From the Holy Spirit came this message: "Set apart Barnabas and Saul for the work to which I have called them."

There was no mistaking what God wanted. These two men, who had been such a help to the Antioch church, were now to go and preach the good tidings of Jesus' love to others.

This was something new in those days, and I imagine there was no little excitement as plans were laid for the great adventure. The church members could talk of nothing else. Their beloved pastors, with young John Mark, a cousin of Barnabas', as their assistant, were going to travel hundreds of miles to establish other Christian churches on the island of Cyprus and all through Asia Minor! How big and important it must have seemed to them then!

At last came the farewell meeting when, after fasting and praying, they laid their hands on them and sent them off. I am sure that crowds went down to the docks at Seleucia to wave good-by as the ship sailed out of the harbor. Mothers and fathers, boys and girls, were all there for the great occasion. Yet, as they shed their tears and shouted their last good wishes, I wonder whether any of them realized that those three lonely figures standing on the deck of that little vessel were the first of a long, long line of missionaries who would go overseas to preach the gospel.

A few hours later the travelers arrived at Salamis, a port on the east coast of Cyprus. As soon as they had found a place to stay they went first to one synagogue, then to another, telling the story of Jesus to the Jewish leaders. Then they journeyed on across the island until they came to the city of Paphos on the west coast. Here they ran into quite a little excitement.

After they had been in town awhile Sergius Paulus, the Roman proconsul, sent for them. He was curious about these strangers and the things they were talking about. He wanted them to explain their message to him. This they were glad to do, and he, an intelligent man, became much interested. Barnabas and Saul could see that he was on the verge of accepting Jesus as his Saviour.

Then came an interruption.

"Don't believe them!" cried a sneering voice. "What they are saying is all nonsense."

It was Elymas, a local magician, who was keen enough to see that if the proconsul accepted what these preachers were saying he wouldn't want a magician around any more. But he soon wished he had kept quiet.

Saul turned on him with burning words of rebuke. He was angry that anyone should get in God's way like this and try to keep this fine Roman officer out of the kingdom.

"You son of the devil," he said to Elymas, "you enemy of all righteousness, full of all deceit and villainy, will you not stop making crooked the straight paths of the Lord? And now, behold, the hand of the Lord is upon you, and you shall be blind and unable to see the sun for a time."

Barely had Saul spoken when his words came true.

"I can't see! I can't see!" cried Elymas, putting his hands to his eyes.

"Mist and darkness" fell upon him, and "he went about seeking people to lead him by the hand."

Deeply impressed, the proconsul gave his heart to God, "for he was astonished at the teaching of the Lord."

As for Saul, something happened to him too. Just how, we are not told. But from this moment on the Bible calls him Paul. Strangely, this new name was the same as that of his first important convert, Sergius *Paulus*. Perhaps Barnabas, equally amazed at what had taken place in the proconsul's house, gave it to him. For Paul means "little." And here was a man little in stature, little in his own sight, but oh, how mighty in the power of God!

STORY 2

Mistaken for Gods

SAILING from Paphos, the three missionaries reached the mainland again at Perga in Asia Minor. Here John Mark said good-by to Paul and Barnabas and left for home. Maybe he got too sick on that last boat trip, or perhaps he couldn't stand the hardships of travel in those days. Anyway, he packed up and returned to Jerusalem, much to Paul's annoyance.

The two older men now went on alone and came to Antioch in Pisidia. Invited to speak in the synagogue, Paul preached a great sermon, proving that Jesus is not only the Son of David but the Son of God. "Through this man," he declared, "is preached unto you the forgiveness of sins."

After the meeting the Gentiles outside asked him to preach the same sermon to them. He did. "And the next sabbath day came almost the whole city together to hear the word of God."

This upset the Jews. They didn't want to share anything

69

JOURNEYS of the APOSTLE PAUL
34-66 A.D.

First Journey ●●●●●●●
Second Journey ----
Third Journey ——
Rome ━━━

PHILIPPI

AS...
ASSOS
...ENE
SMYRNA
EPHESUS
MILETUS
COS
CNIDUS
RHODES

ADRAMYTTIUM
DORYLAEUM

ASIA MINOR

ANTIOCH
ICONIUM
PERGA
LYSTRA
ATTALIA
DERBE
PATARA
MYRA
TARSUS
SELEUCIA
ANTIOCH
DAMASCUS

PAPHOS
SALAMIS
CYPRUS

SIDON
TYRE
PTOLEMAIS
CAESAREA

SEA

ANTIPATRIS
JOPPA
JERUSALEM
GAZA

EGYPT

with the Gentiles. Not even a good preacher. So they became angry with Paul and Barnabas and began to find fault with them and their message.

In the midst of the hubbub Paul said to them, "It was necessary that the word of God should first have been spoken to you: but seeing you put it from you, and judge yourselves unworthy of everlasting life, lo, we turn to the Gentiles."

This pleased the Gentiles, and many of them accepted Jesus as their Saviour. But the Jews stirred up so much trouble that Paul and Barnabas finally had to leave town.

Now the two missionaries went to Iconium and started all over again. Soon this city too was stirred from one end to the other. A great many people, both Jews and Gentiles, became Christians. But this annoyed the others who didn't join the church, and soon the whole place was divided between those who were for the visiting preachers and those who were against them.

Things got so bad that after a while a plot was laid to take their lives. Learning of it in time, Paul and Barnabas left for Lystra, where they preached in peace for a while. Here they brought to Jesus a young man called Timothy, whose mother Eunice and grandmother Lois were already believers.

Then one day as Paul was speaking he noticed a cripple in the audience. The poor man had been lame from birth, and as he listened to the story of the love and power of Jesus he looked up longingly and hopefully. Guessing what was going on in the man's mind, and "seeing that he had faith to be made well," Paul called to him in a loud voice, "Stand upright on your feet!"

Instantly the man "sprang up and walked," to the utter amazement of everybody around.

Like wildfire the report of the miracle spread through town. People by hundreds came running to see the healed cripple and the men who had made him well.

"The gods are come down to us in the likeness of men!" they cried. "And they called Barnabas, Jupiter; and Paul, Mercury, because he was the chief speaker."

Then the priest of the temple of Jupiter "brought oxen and garlands" and prepared to offer sacrifices to the two visiting "gods."

Paul and Barnabas were shocked. The last thing they wanted was to be worshiped as pagan deities!

73

Running into the crowd, they cried, "Don't do this! We
are not gods! We are only men, just like you. We have come
to tell you about the living God, who made heaven and earth,
and the sea and all that is in them; who gives the rain and
the seasons and satisfies your hearts with food and gladness."

"With these words," the Bible says, "they scarcely re-
strained the people from offering sacrifice to them."

At last the people saw that they had been mistaken. Gradually the shouting died down, and the priests took the oxen
and garlands back to their temple.

In place of the excitement came disappointment. Those
who had been loudest in their praise of Paul and Barnabas
now began to find fault with them.

Unfortunately, some travelers arrived from Antioch and
Iconium and, catching sight of the two missionaries, began to

say they were frauds and impostors. This was all the crowd needed to turn once more into a howling mob. Now, instead of wanting to worship Paul and Barnabas, the people thirsted for their blood.

Barnabas escaped, but Paul was stoned.

Supposing him to be dead, they dragged him out of the gates and left his poor, bruised body on the city dump.

But it took more than this to kill Paul. As some of the new believers gathered around to pay their last respects, he opened his eyes, stood up, and went right back into Lystra! What courage! What holy boldness!

No pagan god was Paul, but truly a God-filled man.

STORY 3

Big Argument Settled

NEXT day, having found Barnabas, Paul set off for the nearby city of Derbe. After working here for a while the two returned to Lystra, then to Iconium, and so back to Antioch in Pisidia.

In each of these cities they met with the new disciples, urging them to "continue in the faith" and explaining to them how the kingdom of God is entered "through much tribulation." They also ordained elders in every church and prayed with them.

So they returned to Perga and sailed from the nearby port of Attalia to Seleucia and so to Antioch in Syria, whence they had started out. You can see where they went by looking at the map on pages 70, 71.

What a welcome they received! The whole church came together to hear their report. Those who had waved good-by to them some months before now listened eagerly as the two missionaries "rehearsed all that God had done with them, and how He had opened the door of faith unto the Gentiles."

They had traveled about 2,400 miles in all, which was a long way in those days. And what a story they had to tell! Everybody was thrilled as they heard about Sergius Paulus and Elymas, about the poor cripple at Lystra, about Paul and Barnabas being mistaken for gods, about Paul being stoned and left for dead and how he had got up and walked into the city.

Best of all was the news that the preaching of the gospel had done its life-changing work as wonderfully in one place as another and had touched the hearts of Gentiles and Jews alike. No doubt many a boy and girl in the congregation said, "When I grow up I'm going to be a missionary too."

By and by Paul and Barnabas decided to go to Jerusalem and tell their story to the believers there. On the way they stopped at various churches "declaring the conversion of the Gentiles: and they caused great joy unto all the brethren."

Arriving at Jerusalem, they were given another warm welcome by the church, the apostles and elders, "and they declared all things that God had done with them."

Strangely, not all who listened to them were pleased with their report. Some argued that before Gentiles could become Christians they must become like Jews and keep all the laws that Moses gave the Israelites in the wilderness.

"No!" said Paul, putting his foot down. "That's all wrong. Christ does not require any such thing of His disciples."

The two views were so strongly held that at last the apostles called a big committee meeting to talk it over. It was the first general council of the Christian church.

James was the chairman, and he gave the members all the time they needed to say what was on their hearts. Then Peter got up and reminded the assembly how God had poured out His Holy Spirit upon both Jews and Gentiles alike and put no difference between them. "We believe that through the grace of the Lord Jesus Christ we shall be saved," he said, "even as they."

Then Barnabas and Paul told their story, "what miracles and wonders God had wrought among the Gentiles by them."

When they had finished James gave the final decision: "My judgment," he said, "is that we should not trouble those of the Gentiles who turn to God, but should write to them to abstain from the pollutions of idols and from unchastity and from what is strangled and from blood."

A letter, bearing this message, was then prepared and sent out to the churches.

It was a great forward step. Not only did it settle a big argument, but it opened wide the doors of the Christian church to everybody. From now on men and women among every race and tribe around the globe would know they were welcome. Membership was as free as the love of God.

STORY 4

Singing in Jail

SOMETIME after Paul and Barnabas had returned to Antioch the idea came to them to revisit the churches they had raised up in Asia Minor.

Said Paul: "Come, let us return and visit the brethren in every city where we proclaimed the word of the Lord, and see how they are."

Barnabas said he would be happy to go, and that it would be nice to take John Mark along too, as they had before.

"John Mark!" objected Paul. "Not that boy! He may be your cousin, but I'd never take *him* again. He got scared and ran home."

"Let's give him another chance!" pleaded Barnabas, the "son of encouragement."

"No!" said Paul, *"not* John Mark."

How long they argued we do not know, but the Bible says that "the contention was so sharp between them," that they separated.

It was a pity, for the churches would have loved to see both of them again. But Barnabas would not desert his young cousin, and so sailed with him to Cyprus. As for Paul, he chose Silas as his new companion, and "went through Syria and Cilicia, confirming the churches."

As it turned out, Barnabas was right. John Mark proved to be a valuable and trustworthy laborer. In later years even Paul came to speak of him as a fellow worker "unto the kingdom of God" and "a comfort unto me" (Colossians 4:10, 11). And just before his death he wrote: "He is profitable to me for the ministry" (2 Timothy 4:11).

So it pays to give boys—and girls—another chance!

Journeying on from church to church, Paul and Silas came to Lystra, where Paul had been stoned and left for dead on his previous trip. Among those waiting to welcome him were young Timothy, his mother, Eunice, and his grandmother, Lois, who had accepted Jesus when he was there before. How glad they must have been to see him again! Yes, and how glad Paul must have been that he went to Lystra in the first place, despite all he suffered there. Had he not done so, this lovely family would never have become Christians.

Eager to spread the gospel ever farther and farther, Paul tried to enter other parts of Asia Minor, but for one reason or another he was unable to do so. There was always something in the way. He wondered why. Then one night he found out.

80

SINGING IN JAIL

He was at Troas, a port on the Aegean Sea, from which place ships left constantly for various ports of Europe. As he slept he saw in vision a man dressed in the costume of the Macedonians, who said, "Come over into Macedonia, and help us."

In the morning Paul told Silas what he had seen and heard, and they both took it to be a call from God. That very day they went down to the docks and booked passage on a ship going to Neapolis. Arriving there, they disembarked and made their way to Philippi, which at that time was "the chief city of that part of Macedonia."

There they stayed, looking for opportunity to win someone to Christ.

Learning that some of the pious women of the church went every Sabbath to a place of prayer by the river, they decided to go and worship with them. As a result Lydia, a "seller of purple" cloth, accepted Jesus as her Saviour and was baptized. She then invited Paul and Silas to stay in her home, which they were glad to do.

This led to the conversion of another woman, and lots of trouble.

One day, as Paul and Silas were on their way to the prayer meeting, a slave girl passed by calling out, "These men are servants of the Most High God, who proclaim to you the way of salvation."

The two men were astonished. How did this poor, uneducated girl know so much? But as she kept on saying the same words over and over again they decided that she must be possessed by an evil spirit. She was, in fact, a soothsayer, and made much money for her owners by her supposed power to read the mind and foretell the future.

Stopping the girl, Paul spoke to the evil spirit, saying, "I charge you in the name of Jesus Christ to come out of her." The spirit obeyed, and the girl was left in her right mind, thankful to be free again.

SINGING IN JAIL

But her owners weren't thankful. They were angry. See-ing their hope of easy money taken from them, they rushed Paul and Silas to the local magistrates, charging them with being troublemakers and teaching customs offensive to the Roman people.

There was no fair trial. Paul and Silas had no chance to defend themselves. In no time at all everybody was shout-ing insults at them. The magistrates judged them guilty and ordered that they should be beaten and put in jail.

So their clothes were torn off them and they were publicly beaten and taken to prison. Here they were placed in the inner-most dungeon, their feet being fastened in the stocks.

It was enough to crush anybody's spirit. But not Paul's or Silas'. They might have asked, "Why did God let this happen to us when we were working for Him?" But they didn't. Instead, despite the pain of their bruised and bleeding backs, they "prayed and sang praises unto God." Hearing their happy voices, the other prisoners marveled.

Singing in jail! What a thing to do! No grumbling, only thanksgiving. What wonderful men they must have been! No wonder God loved them so. No wonder He shook the earth to set them free!

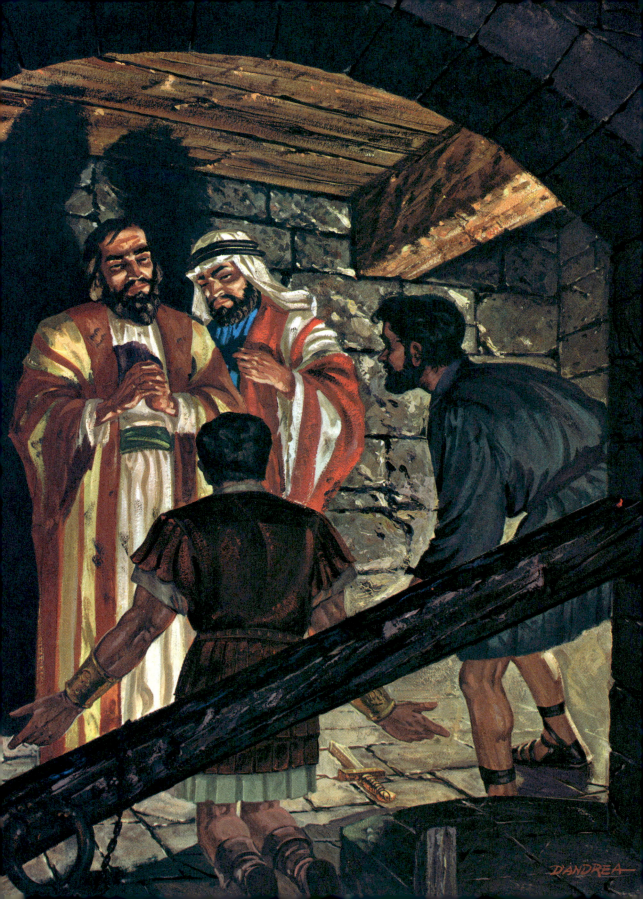

STORY 5

The Wound Washer

SUDDENLY, at midnight, while Paul and Silas were still singing, "there was a great earthquake, so that the foundations of the prison were shaken: and immediately all the doors were opened, and every one's bands were loosed."

Awaking from sleep, the head jailer rushed from his bed to find out what had happened. In the murky darkness he couldn't see much—just piles of debris on the floor and the dungeon doors swinging wide open.

Fearing that his prisoners had run away, and knowing he would be blamed for their escape, he drew his sword and was about to kill himself when Paul cried out, "Don't harm yourself. We are all here."

"A light!" cried the jailer. "Bring a light!"

A servant came running with a torch. Then the jailer made his way into the inner dungeon and fell on his knees before Paul and Silas.

Having heard these men praying and singing, he knew

85

Although Paul and Silas had been arrested for preaching and healing in the name of Jesus, God sent a great earthquake that shook down the doors, delivering them from their jailers.

in his heart that they had been wrongfully beaten and jailed. He knew, too, that they had something he did not have—a peace of mind he wanted but had never known.

Now as he led them out of the dungeon he said, "Men, what must I do to be saved?"

This was a most unusual question for a jailer to ask of his prisoners, but Paul was ready with an answer. He saw another chance to tell the gospel story.

"Believe in the Lord Jesus," he said, "and you will be saved, you and your household."

The man knew little or nothing about Jesus. So he took Paul and Silas into his home that he might learn what they meant by these strange words.

The two preachers weren't very presentable. Their clothes were torn, their backs bloodstained, their hands unwashed, their beards untidy. So the jailer did his best to fix them up and make them comfortable, while Paul and Silas went on talking.

First of all, he washed their wounds. That was a beautiful thing for him to do. He wanted to make right the wrong that had been done to these good men, and this was the best way he knew of doing it.

What a wonderful lesson there is for us here! If we wound somebody by word or deed, it's not enough just to say, "I'm sorry." We must wash the wounds and do what we can to make them better.

Boys and girls are often all too quick to wound others, and all too slow to wash the wounds they make. They will gang up on other boys or girls at school and make fun of their clothes, their lunch, their parents, or perhaps their color, never thinking of the wounds they cause or the need for someone to heal them. Sometimes cruel things are said or done at home, with a little brother or sister feeling the "stripes" of unkindness in his heart.

The world needs more wound washers today. So does your church, your school, your family.

By morning light the jailer of Philippi had been baptized, together with his wife and children. What a night that was! It began with a beating and ended with a baptism, with an earthquake thrown in for good measure.

Then the police arrived with a message from the magis-

trates to say that Paul and Silas were now free to leave the prison.

"Oh, no," said Paul. "They have beaten us publicly, uncondemned, men who are Roman citizens, and have thrown us into prison; and do they now cast us out secretly? No! let them come themselves and take us out."

Now it was the magistrates' turn to be worried. To beat a Roman citizen without a proper trial was a serious offense in those days. On learning what Paul had said they came hurrying to the prison to apologize. Politely they begged the two men to leave town as soon as possible.

Paul and Silas accepted the apology, but they were in no hurry to leave Philippi. From the prison they went to see their friend Lydia and to talk with the other new believers. Then, in their own good time, they went on their way to Thessalonica, where more exciting events awaited them.

STORY 6

Turning the World Upside Down

FROM Philippi, Paul and Silas made their way to Thessalonica, or Salonika as it is called today. This meant a journey of about a hundred miles and probably took several days, allowing for stops on the way.

By the time the two missionaries arrived in Thessalonica they had recovered from the bad beating they had been given in jail and were all ready to preach again.

After finding lodging in the home of a man called Jason they went to the synagogue and "Paul went in, as was his custom, and for three weeks he argued with them from the scriptures, explaining and proving that it was necessary for the Christ to suffer and to rise from the dead, and saying, 'This Jesus, whom I proclaim to you, is the Christ.' "

For a while all went well. Some Jews believed and accepted Jesus as their Saviour. Many Greeks believed also, "and not a few of the leading women."

Paul and Silas must have been very happy at this fine

result of their preaching. But their joy did not last very long. Soon some of the Jews, who refused to believe that Jesus was the Messiah, charged that the two men were frauds and cheats and should be driven out of town. Gathering a crowd, they "set the city in an uproar."

Arriving at Jason's house, they demanded that Paul and Silas should be handed over to them. But the apostles weren't there. Perhaps they had slipped out the back door when they saw the angry crowd coming down the street.

Angered because they couldn't find the men they were looking for, the leaders of the mob seized Jason and rushed him off to the city magistrates.

"These men who have turned the world upside down have come here also," they cried. "And Jason has received them; and they are all acting against the decrees of Caesar, saying that there is another king, Jesus."

There was a good deal of fuss and argument, but finally Jason was set free after he had put up a bond for his good behavior. Returning home, he got word to Paul and Silas that it would be best for them to leave town for a while. That night the two set out for Berea, some fifty miles toward the west.

As they trudged on through the darkness they must have smiled as they thought of what their enemies had said about them that day. I can almost hear Paul saying, "So they think we are turning the world upside down! I wish we were!"

TURNING THE WORLD UPSIDE DOWN

It didn't seem like it at the moment. Once more they were running for their lives, looking back now and then to see whether they were being pursued, and wondering whether they would get safely to Berea.

True, a good many people had accepted their message in Thessalonica, but how few they were compared with the crowds who had rejected it! Both of them wished they might have stayed longer and done a greater work. It was too bad they had had to leave so soon. As for turning the world upside down, nothing seemed more impossible or absurd.

Yet that is exactly what they were doing. Day after day, in city after city, they were planting ideas in people's minds that would change their lives completely. They would be turned upside down, and so would the world in which they lived.

That's what the gospel of Jesus does. It turns people upside down—and inside out. It changes their likes and dislikes. It changes their motives and ambitions. Instead of loving the world and hating God they love God and hate the world. Instead of being selfish they become unselfish. Instead of being proud they become humble. Instead of being irritable they become patient. Instead of seeking to please themselves they try their best to please Jesus. Their whole outlook on life is changed. Their world is turned upside down.

And that's what Jesus will do for you, if you receive Him into your heart.

STORY 7

Seekers After Truth

ARRIVING in Berea, Paul and Silas began once more to preach about Jesus and here they ran across something that greatly cheered their hearts.

As they spoke in the synagogue they noticed that the people were most eager to learn the truth. The ancient scrolls were brought out and examined with great care. The Bible says that "these Jews were more noble than those in Thessalonica, for they received the word with all eagerness, examining the scriptures daily to see if these things were so."

No doubt there were meetings in the people's homes as well as in the synagogue. Everywhere there was earnest Bible study. As a result many believed, "with not a few Greek women of high standing as well as men."

When word got back to Thessalonica about what was happening, the Jews who had caused trouble there hurried over to Berea and tried to undo the good work the Christian missionaries had begun. To avoid trouble Paul went to Athens, leaving

93

The Bereans were more responsive to the gospel than the people of Thessalonica because they recognized the authority of God's Word and studied its counsels daily for instruction.

Silas and Timothy to strengthen the new disciples in the faith.

Taking ship, Paul sailed for the famous capital of Greece, which he had often longed to see. But he was disappointed. The city was full of idols, and nobody took much notice of his preaching.

"What has this babbler got to say?" they asked with a sneer. As Paul tried to argue with them they laughed at him.

On Mars' Hill, where the people of Athens gathered to discuss the news, he tried to interest them in the greatest news of all—that the invisible God had made Himself visible in Jesus, and that, though He had been crucified by wicked men, He had risen from the dead. This Jesus, he said, was alive and would one day "judge the world in righteousness."

94

The result was disappointing. "When they heard of the resurrection of the dead, some mocked; but others said, 'We will hear you again about this.'" Only a very few believed.

So Paul went on to Corinth, no doubt wondering whether he would have the same experience in that big city as he had had in Athens.

Arriving in town, he made the acquaintance of a Jew named Aquila and his wife, Priscilla. They were tentmakers, and since this was Paul's trade too, they were soon good friends.

As usual Paul began his work by visiting the synagogues, but he had a hard time. Fierce arguments developed. So bitterly was he opposed that at last he said to the Jewish leaders, "Your blood be upon your heads! I am innocent. From now on I will go to the Gentiles."

It was most discouraging. Paul must have asked himself many times whether it was worth while going on trying to preach the gospel to such people. Then one night the Lord Jesus spoke to him in a vision. "Do not be afraid," He said, "but speak and do not be silent; for I am with you, and no man shall attack you to harm you; for I have many people in this city."

Greatly cheered, Paul stayed on in Corinth for another eighteen months, "teaching the word of God."

And the Lord kept His promise. Many people accepted Paul's message, and the Corinthian church was formed. When trouble finally came and the Jews made a "united attack" upon Paul he was protected from harm by the chief magistrate.

As he stood before the Roman proconsul Gallio, charged with "persuading men to worship God contrary to the law" he must have wondered whether he would be condemned or released. But the Lord had said he would not be harmed in Corinth, and he wasn't.

Turning upon the men who had brought the charge against Paul, Gallio said, " 'If it were a matter of wrongdoing or vicious crime, I should have reason to bear with you, O Jews; but since it is a matter of questions about words and names and your own law, see to it yourselves; I refuse to be a judge of these things.' And he drove them from the tribunal."

So Paul was released and, bidding good-by to the new Corinthian Christians, he left by ship for Syria, taking with him his good friends the tentmakers, Aquila and Priscilla.

After a brief visit to the church at Ephesus where he left his two friends, he sailed on to Caesarea. From here he went by road to Jerusalem, and then back to his old home church at Antioch. What a story he had to tell when he got there!

STORY 8

Seven Foolish Boys

AFTER spending some time in Antioch, Paul became restless again. He wanted to visit the churches he had raised up on his two previous missionary journeys. So "he departed and went from place to place through the region of Galatia and Phrygia, strengthening all the disciples."

How glad the new believers must have been to see him again! For there was no radio then, no television, no daily mail service by which they might receive a message of cheer from their beloved leader. Only on the rarest occasions could they hope to receive a letter from him. Seldom, if ever, did they hear any preacher other than their own church elder. Now here was Paul among them again in person! I am sure they welcomed him with tears of joy.

In the course of his travels Paul came again to Ephesus. Here wonderful things began to happen. For three months he spoke in the synagogue "arguing and pleading about the kingdom of God." Then, when some in his audience became troublesome, he rented the hall of Tyrannus and spoke there every day for two years. Thousands came to hear him, for we read that "all the residents of Asia heard the word of the Lord, both Jews and Greeks."

And it was not only Paul's preaching that impressed the people so much. They were amazed at the way he healed the sick. The Bible tells us that "God did extraordinary miracles by the hands of Paul, so that handkerchiefs or aprons were carried away from his body to the sick, and diseases left them, and the evil spirits came out of them."

In the audience one day were seven boys—the seven sons of a Jewish priest named Sceva. They noticed that whenever Paul spoke to some poor sick man or woman and said, "In the name of Jesus Christ of Nazareth, be well"—or words like that—the sick person was made better immediately. So, thinking there must be some magic in Paul's words, they decided to find out whether the same words would "work" for them.

Seeing a man in the crowd who evidently was possessed by an evil spirit, one of them said to him, "I adjure you by the Jesus whom Paul preaches"—and bade the spirit depart.

Nothing happened. At least, nothing that the boys expected. Instead "the evil spirit answered them, 'Jesus I know, and Paul I know; but who are you?'" Whereupon the wild man leaped on them, tore their clothes off them, and knocked them about so badly that they fled in terror, "naked and wounded."

Those seven boys learned a lesson that day which I am sure they never forgot. Never again did they use the precious name of Jesus in jest, or as if it were a conjurer's magic word.

SEVEN FOOLISH BOYS

That there is power in His name I gladly agree. But that power is revealed only when His name is used reverently and sincerely by one who loves the Lord with a perfect heart.

The devil feared Jesus and Paul, but he wasn't the least bit afraid of the seven sons of Sceva. They had no Christian experience. No power from heaven was flowing through their lives. They were just seven silly boys playing with religion.

That makes me think. Is the devil afraid of me? Is he afraid of you?

STORY 9

Bonfire in Ephesus

WHENEVER someone bears a bold witness for Jesus you may be sure it won't be long before Satan stages a counterattack.

So it was in Ephesus. Paul's witness there was greatly blessed. Hundreds accepted Jesus. When they did so they threw away their idols and gave up all the worldly pleasures on which they once had wasted their time and money.

The Bible says that "a number of those who practiced magic arts brought their books together and burned them in the sight of all; and they counted the value of them and found it came to fifty thousand pieces of silver. So the word of the Lord grew and prevailed mightily."

What a bonfire that must have been!

Seeing his own books burned was more than the devil could take. So he moved upon a man named Demetrius to cause trouble for Paul and the new Christians.

This man was a silversmith, whose chief source of in-

BONFIRE IN EPHESUS

come came from making silver shrines for Diana—or Artemis —the famous goddess of Ephesus. Gradually it dawned on him that if Paul's teachings spread much farther there wouldn't be anybody left to buy his little silver shrines and idols.

So he called a meeting of fellow silversmiths and said to them, "Men, you know that from this business we have our wealth. And you see and hear that not only at Ephesus but almost throughout all Asia this Paul has persuaded and turned away a considerable company of people, saying that gods made with hands are not gods. And there is danger not only that this trade of ours may come into disrepute but also that the temple of the great goddess Artemis [or Diana] may count for nothing, and that she may even be deposed from her magnificence, she whom all Asia and the world worship."

Demetrius put a lot of fire into his speech, and by the time he had finished his friends were all stirred up. "Great is Diana of the Ephesians!" they cried. "Great is Artemis of the Ephesians!"

Pretty soon they were running through the city, shouting the same slogans until the whole city was "filled with confusion." Grabbing two of Paul's companions, they rushed with them into the great open-air theater.

Learning of what had happened, Paul wanted to go too, but his friends wouldn't let him, fearing that he might be torn to pieces.

Meanwhile, the crowd continued to pour into the theater until it was packed to the topmost tier. But not all who came knew why the meeting had been called. "Some therefore cried one thing, and some another." Then for two hours they chanted in unison, "Great is Diana of the Ephesians!"

When at last they grew tired the town clerk managed to get everybody quiet enough to listen to him. He spoke some flattering words about the great goddess Diana, then added the warning, "We are in danger of being charged with rioting today, there being no cause we can give to justify this commotion."

Slowly the people began to file out of the theater. When everybody had gone home and the uproar had ceased, Paul called the church members together and told them he thought it was time for him to leave. They were saddened by his words, but saw good reason in them. So he bade them farewell and set out for Macedonia and Greece.

STORY 10

The Boy Who Slept in Church

I T HAPPENED at a place called Troas on the coast of Asia Minor. Paul had just returned from Greece, where he had gone to encourage the new believers.

After spending a week with the Christians in Troas, he had met with them again on the first day of the week in an "upper chamber" on the third story of some local building.

The grand old missionary had no doubt already preached in the morning and perhaps again Sabbath afternoon. Then, "on the first day of the week" which, in those days, began at sunset Saturday night, he held yet another meeting. He wanted to celebrate the Lord's Supper before leaving in the morning.

Nobody knows the exact hour when this meeting began, but we do know when it was interrupted and when it finally ended.

Paul had so much to say and so many wonderful stories to tell that he "prolonged his speech until midnight."

103

How many people dozed during that long, long service we are not told, but the name of the boy who went fast asleep will never be forgotten.

Eutychus was "sitting in the window" and "sank down into a deep sleep as Paul talked still longer."

Evidently the window was open, for the poor lad fell out and hit the ground with a fearful thud three stories down.

You can imagine the commotion. Paul was forgotten. Women screamed, and men rushed outside to see what had happened.

Everybody was wide awake now as the word was passed from one to another, "Eutychus fell out of the window, and he's dead."

A lantern held high in someone's hand showed where the body lay, and a crowd quickly gathered around it. Nobody could see much in the dim light.

Then Paul came striding through. Pressing his way to the front, he knelt down beside Eutychus and put his arms about him, much as Elisha, long years before, had embraced the dead son of the Shunammite woman.

After a few moments he stood up again. "Don't worry," he said. "He is alive."

Everybody was amazed. They couldn't understand it. But there was no doubt that what Paul said was true.

Some of the members picked the boy up and took him home, "and were not a little comforted."

You might think that this would have brought the meeting to a close. Oh, no! After a little break Paul went right back to the pulpit and carried on from where he had left off. The Bible says that when he had gone upstairs again and "had broken bread and eaten, he conversed with them a long while, until daybreak, and so departed."

What happened to Eutychus afterward we are not told. But when he grew up and heard his friends talking about that wonderful night when the apostle Paul preached in his church, he must always have had a feeling of regret. That was the greatest night in the history of Troas, and he knew nothing about it! He had slept through it all! It doesn't pay to sleep in church.

STORY 11

Sermon on the Stairs

ONE cannot but admire the energy and stamina of the apostle Paul. After preaching all night he set out at daybreak for Assos, nineteen miles away, where his friends, who had sailed around the peninsula by ship, planned to pick him up. That was quite a walk for a Sunday morning!

When he arrived at Assos the ship was waiting for him. It was a small vessel, which put in at various seaside cities along the coast of Asia Minor. On reaching Miletus, Paul sent a messenger to Ephesus, asking the elders of the church there to come and see him. They came gladly and spent several precious hours with him.

Feeling sure that he would never pass this way again, Paul gave them much good advice, commending them to God and "to the word of His grace."

"And when he had spoken thus, he knelt down and prayed with them all." And the record says "they all wept" and embraced him "and kissed him, sorrowing most of all because of the word he had spoken, that they should see his face no more."

As the ship sailed out of the harbor Paul stood on the deck, waving a last farewell to his friends on the shore. I am sure there were tears running down his cheeks as he called to them, "Good-by, good-by, God bless you!"

Then the wind caught the sails, and the ship rounded the point and was gone.

Some days later the party arrived at Tyre and spent a week with the church there. When it came time to leave, every member, including the wives and children, came to see them off. Kneeling on the beach, they prayed together and bade each other farewell. It must have been a very touching sight, especially when Paul shook hands with the boys and girls. I can see them looking up at him with tear-dimmed eyes, so sad to think he would never come back again.

From Tyre it was but a short trip to Caesarea, where Paul and his friends went ashore. After a considerable stay they made their way to Jerusalem. Here the church leaders gave them a warm welcome. Then Paul "related one by one the things that God had done among the Gentiles through his ministry."

It was a great story, and "when they heard it, they glorified God."

Then Paul went to the Temple. He was glad to see the familiar old building again after all his travels. And it was good to walk among the crowds that had flocked into the Temple court for the feast of Pentecost. But how he wished these thousands would all accept Jesus as their Saviour! It was sad to think that twenty-five years after the Holy Spirit had come upon the disciples in this very city so many people still refused to listen to the gospel.

Suddenly he was recognized by some Jews who had opposed his work in the cities of Asia Minor.

At once there was trouble.

"Men of Israel, help!" they cried. "This is the man who is teaching men everywhere against the people and the law and this place; moreover he has also brought Greeks into the temple and he has defiled this holy place."

The charge wasn't true, but it was enough to start a riot.

Paul was seized and dragged out of the Temple court and the gates were shut. Outside, more and more people came together, all shouting abuse at him and trying to strike him.

No doubt Paul would have been killed there and then but for the fact that a company of Roman soldiers suddenly appeared on the scene and subdued the anger of the mob.

"What's going on here?" asked the captain. "Why are you beating this man?"

Some shouted one thing, some another, and the captain, thinking Paul must be some terrible criminal, ordered that he be bound with chains and taken to the barracks.

On the way Paul spoke to the captain and tried to clear things up.

"Aren't you the leader of a band of assassins?" asked the captain.

"No, indeed!" Paul assured him. "I am a Jew, from Tarsus in Cilicia, a citizen of no mean city; I beg of you, let me speak to the people."

Impressed by Paul's cultured speech and manner, the captain agreed. So, standing on the stairs leading up to the barracks, Paul "motioned with his hand to the people." Astonished at the turn of events, they became quiet, wondering what this manacled prisoner would have to say.

"Brethren and fathers," he cried in the language of the people, "hear the defense which I now make before you." Then he went on to tell his life story from his birth to his conversion on the Damascus road. All went well until he said that the Lord had told him to go and preach to the Gentiles.

This was too much for his listeners.

"Away with such a fellow from the earth!" they yelled, waving their garments and throwing dust in the air.

So great was the din that Paul's voice was completely drowned. Fearing worse trouble, the captain moved his men up the steps and into the barracks. Then he gave orders that Paul should be flogged.

"Is it lawful for you to scourge a man that is a Roman citizen, and uncondemned?" Paul asked the centurion who was about to beat him.

Going to the captain, the centurion said, "You'd better be careful, sir; this man is a Roman citizen."

Worried, the captain went to Paul.

"Are you a Roman?" he asked.

"Yes," said Paul.

"With a great sum obtained I this freedom," the officer said.

"But I was free born," Paul replied.

A few hours later his chains were removed.

STORY 12

Boy With a Secret

≈≈≈≈≈≈≈≈≈≈≈≈≈≈≈≈

NEXT day the captain ordered the chief priests and their council to meet and listen to Paul's defense. They agreed, and Paul was taken to the meeting, which proved to be a very stormy one.

Scarcely had the apostle begun to speak when "a great clamor arose." Some took his part, others opposed him. The room was filled with angry shouts. Finally the captain, "afraid that Paul would be torn to pieces by them, commanded the soldiers to go down and take him by force from among them and bring him into the barracks."

So the Romans saved Paul's life again. But he was discouraged. He had had a wonderful opportunity to witness before the Jewish leaders, and it seemed as if he had spoiled it. But Jesus knew he had done his best, and the next night "the Lord stood by him and said, 'Take courage, for as you have testified about me in Jerusalem, so you must bear witness also at Rome.'"

This cheered his heart, for he had always wanted to see Rome, and now he knew that his life would be spared until this dream came true.

A short time later a boy knocked on the door of the barracks and asked permission to see Paul. "He's my uncle," he said, "and I have a message for him."

The boy proved to be Paul's sister's son, his own nephew. "What news do you bring me?" asked Paul.

Excitedly the boy told his story. He had learned of a plot that had been laid to take his uncle's life. About forty men had sworn not to eat or drink until they had killed him. They had asked the chief priests to ask the captain to bring Paul to the council again. They planned to murder him on the way.

"Very interesting," I can hear Paul saying. "Thank you. Would you please tell this to the captain?"

BOY WITH A SECRET

"Certainly," said the boy, anxious to save his uncle's life.

This he did, and the captain believed him. After telling the boy to keep his secret well, he ordered two of his centurions to get ready "two hundred soldiers with seventy horsemen and two hundred spearmen" to take Paul to Caesarea and deliver him to Governor Felix.

That was quite a lot of men to look after one Christian preacher, but the captain was determined that no harm should come to him while he was in his charge.

After dark that night the soldiers set off on their journey. As they clattered out of the gates of Jerusalem nobody dreamed that the cloaked figure on horseback in the middle was the apostle Paul. Nobody, that is, except Paul's nephew. I think he must have guessed. And I am sure he chuckled as he thought of those forty men who had sworn to kill Paul. If they kept their oath, they would go hungry for a long, long time.

STORY 13

Heaven Missed by Inches

JESUS told His disciples that they would be brought "before governors and kings" for His sake, and this certainly came true in the life of the apostle Paul.

Shortly after arriving in Caesarea he was brought before Governor Felix. Felix knew a good deal about the Christian faith, and he and his wife, Drusilla, had many talks with him. Once, as Paul spoke about "justice and self-control and future judgment," Felix became alarmed and said, "Go away for the present; when I have an opportunity I will call you."

At that moment Felix was very close to accepting Jesus as his Saviour, but he put off his decision to "a more convenient season"—which never came. How near he was to the kingdom! How sad that he drew back! So near and yet so far!

After two years Felix was transferred to another post and "desiring to do the Jews a favor, left Paul in prison."

Festus, the new governor, ordered Paul to be brought before him so that he might find out for himself why this man

114

had been kept in prison so long. He, too, treated Paul kindly, asking him whether he would like to go to Jerusalem for his trial. Paul said No. "I am standing before Caesar's tribunal, where I ought to be tried," he said; "to the Jews I have done no wrong, as you know very well. If then I am a wrongdoer, and have committed anything for which I deserve to die, I do not seek to escape death; but if there is nothing in their charges against me, no one can give me up to them. I appeal to Caesar."

Festus turned to his councilors and asked for their advice. Then he said to Paul, "You have appealed to Caesar; to Caesar you shall go."

Before Paul could be sent to Rome, however, King Agrippa and his wife, Bernice, arrived in Caesarea. Festus told them about the famous prisoner he had on his hands, and the king said he would like to see him.

So a meeting was arranged. When Paul was brought in King Agrippa told him to go ahead and tell all that was on

his heart. Paul was delighted to have the chance to do so. Once again he told the story of his life and how Jesus had spoken to him on the Damascus road. Then he related how, in obedience to this heavenly vision, he had gone everywhere, declaring that all men, both Jews and Gentiles, "should repent and turn to God and perform deeds worthy of their repentance."

As he explained how Christ fulfilled the Old Testament prophecies about the Messiah he became more and more earnest; so much so that Festus suddenly called to him in a loud voice, "Paul, you are mad; your great learning is turning you mad."

"I am not mad, most excellent Festus," he said, "but I am speaking the sober truth." Then, turning to the king he asked, "King Agrippa, do you believe the prophets? I know that you believe."

"You almost persuade me to be a Christian," said the king.

"Would to God that not only you but also all who hear me this day might become such as I am—except for these chains," said Paul.

At this the meeting broke up, King Agrippa saying to Festus, "This man could have been set free if he had not appealed to Caesar."

That was a great moment in the king's life. He was almost persuaded, but not quite. Like Felix he put off deciding for Christ till another time, and put it off too long.

Like Felix he almost stepped into heaven, only to lose it forever. He missed it by inches, as one might say. Let us be careful lest we do the same.

117

← PAINTING BY HERBERT RUDEEN   ©   BY REVIEW AND HERALD

Chained to his captor, Paul told the story of his conversion to Christ with such courage and earnestness that King Agrippa was deeply moved and almost persuaded to believe.

STORY 14

Angel in the Storm

A S THERE was no ship sailing direct from Caesarea to Rome, Paul, with some other prisoners, was put on board a vessel bound for ports along the coast of Asia. When this ship had gone as far as Myra, all the prisoners were transferred to another ship going to Italy.

What a voyage that was! Trouble began soon after they left port. The winds being unfavorable, the ship traveled slowly, losing valuable days. By the time it reached Crete, winter was coming on, so Paul advised the centurion to anchor there and wait for better weather. "But the centurion paid more attention to the captain than to what Paul said," which was natural, and it was decided to sail on.

The captain was soon sorry he had done so, for a gale sprang up and he could do nothing but let the ship run before it.

Next day the storm became worse, and the captain decided to lighten the ship by throwing much of the cargo overboard. The day after that the tackle was thrown over too.

118

ANGEL IN THE STORM

"And when neither sun nor stars appeared for many a day" all hope of being saved faded away.

By this time most of the prisoners and crew were worn out with hunger, weariness, seasickness, and fear. Many were lying in the filthy hold, helpless, hopeless, and terrified.

Then it was that Paul stood among them, his face alight with courage and hope.

As the ship rolled and tossed about in the mountainous seas he somehow managed to keep his footing as he said, "Men, you should have listened to me, and should not have set sail from Crete and incurred this injury and loss. I now bid you take heart; for there will be no loss of life among you, but only of the ship. For this very night there stood by me an angel of the God to whom I belong and whom I worship, and he said, Do not be afraid, Paul; you must stand before Caesar; and lo, God has granted you all those who sail with you."

So God had heard Paul's prayers for his fellow prisoners and for the crew; for the captain and the centurion.

ANGEL IN THE STORM

Best of all, God had sent him a personal message of comfort, and the angel bearing it had found his way through the fearsome tempest, right into the hold of that storm-tossed vessel! How carefully God watches over His faithful children!

No wonder Paul's heart was full of courage! No wonder he could say to those poor, miserable soldiers and sailors, "Take heart, men, for I have faith in God that it will be exactly as I have told!"

And it did turn out exactly as he said.

A few days later the ship ran aground on the island of Malta and was broken to pieces by the heavy seas.

The soldiers wanted to kill the prisoners, lest they somehow escape, "but the centurion, wishing to save Paul, kept them from carrying out their purpose. He ordered those who could swim to throw themselves overboard first and make for the land, and the rest on planks or on pieces of the ship. And so it was that all escaped to land."

There were 276 people on that ship and everyone was saved, just as Paul had promised.

Right after landing, as Paul was sitting by a fire trying to dry his clothes, a snake struck at him and fastened itself upon his hand. Those who saw this happen expected him to fall dead at once, but instead he calmly shook off the creature and suffered no harm.

The natives were so astonished at this that they felt sure he must be some god, but he told them No, he was only a servant of the God of heaven. Then he went on to prove it by kind words and deeds. After he had healed the father of the chief man of the island "the rest of the people who had diseases also came and were cured." Heaven never drew so close to Malta as it did just then; and when the time came for Paul to leave, everybody was sad to see him go.

After three months on the island the party set sail once more and finally reached Rome. Here, to Paul's surprise, a few Christians came out to meet him, for which he "thanked God and took courage." Then, though bound with a chain, he invited the local Jews to visit him. They came in great numbers to his lodging, and he preached to them about Jesus.

What a man! The Bible says that for two years he preached and taught like this, "openly and unhindered." So he waited to see Caesar and for the martyr's death that lay ahead.

PART III

Stories of the First Christian Letters

All the Bible texts quoted in Part III are from the Revised
Standard Version of the Bible except where indicated otherwise.

(ROMANS 1:1-JUDE 25)

STORY 1

Paul's Love Letters

WHILE Paul was a prisoner in Rome he not only preached the gospel to all who came to visit him but also found time to write letters to the churches he had founded in Macedonia and Asia Minor.

But these are not the only letters Paul wrote. Just how many letters Paul wrote while on his missionary journeys and while in prison, nobody knows. The number must have been far more than the dozen or so that exist today.

He was, in fact, one of the most famous letter writers of all time. Some of his letters are still read every day by millions of people all around the world.

Half of the books of the New Testament were written by him. These "books" are really letters, or "epistles," as they are sometimes called. Some were addressed to churches in cities such as Corinth, Philippi, or Colossae. Others were written to personal friends like Timothy and Titus.

All of Paul's letters were love letters. You can't read them

125

After his eventful missionary journeys Paul was imprisoned in a Roman dungeon, but before he was put to death he wrote letters of encouragement to the churches he had served.

without feeling the love he had for the people to whom he wrote. He counted them all as his own sons and daughters. He had suffered much to bring them the gospel, and they were all very dear to his heart. "You are our glory and joy" he told them, and he meant every word.

Because he loved these new converts so much he sent them much good advice on all sorts of subjects. He was anxious that they should not lack any spiritual gift as they waited for the return of Jesus.

He wanted to make sure that they would stay in the church and not be led away by false teachers. That is why he tried to make the gospel as plain as he could to them. Over and over again he set before them the high standards of conduct that God expected of them as Christians. Times without number he assured them that God by His Holy Spirit would give them power to live noble lives, worthy of their high calling.

Faithfully he warned them that their resolve to be followers of Jesus would bring them into trouble. Enemies would try to harm them. But they were not to worry. To the Romans he had previously written these brave and encouraging words: "Who shall separate us from the love of Christ? Shall tribulation, or distress, or persecution, or famine, or nakedness, or peril, or sword? . . . No, in all these things we are more than conquerors through Him who loved us. For I am sure that neither death, nor life, nor angels, nor principalities, nor things present, nor things to come, nor powers, nor height, nor depth, nor anything else in all creation, will be able to

126

separate us from the love of God in Christ Jesus our Lord."

As you read Paul's love letters you will come across some things that may seem difficult to understand at first. Never mind. Peter felt the same way about them, for he wrote: "There are some things in them hard to understand."

Always try to remember when these letters were written and to whom they were written. They are the oldest Christian letters in existence, having been written between A.D. 50 and 65—not many years after the crucifixion of Christ and only a little while after the new Christians had come out of pagan idolatry or from among the Jews. There was so much truth these dear people needed to know that it took someone with Paul's keen mind and loving heart to explain it all to them.

By studying the "books" of Romans, Corinthians, Thessalonians, and the other epistles you will learn much about the Christian church as it was nineteen hundred years ago and of the love in the heart of the man who did so much to raise it up.

STORY 2

Love at Its Best

HAVE you ever asked yourself what is the meaning of the word "love"?

When you say, "I love my dog," or "I love my pet canary," or "I love my mother," what do you have in mind? Do you mean that you just have a nice friendly feeling inside you toward your dog, your canary, or your mother? Or is love something more than that?

It is really quite important that we know what love is, because it is the most important word in the Bible. "God is love" we are told, and Jesus came from heaven to earth to tell us so. When a lawyer asked Him, "Which is the great commandment in the law?" Jesus replied, *"Thou shalt love* the Lord thy God with all thy heart, and with all thy soul, and with all thy mind. This is the first and great commandment. And the second is like unto it, *Thou shalt love* thy neighbour as thyself" (K.J.V.).

To His disciples Jesus said, "This is my commandment,

128

LOVE AT ITS BEST

That ye love one another, as I have loved you" (K.J.V.).

It is plain, therefore, that if we are going to be true followers of Jesus, we must learn to love and love and keep on loving. But how?

Paul tried to answer this question in his first letter to the church in Corinth. There had been trouble among the members. Some had been jealous. Others had been proud and boastful. All such feelings were wrong, he said, because they were the opposite of love.

"If I speak in the tongues of men and of angels," he said, "but have not love, I am a noisy gong or a clanging cymbal.

"And if I have prophetic powers, and understand all mysteries and all knowledge, and if I have all faith, so as to remove mountains, but have not love, I am nothing.

"If I give away all I have, and if I deliver my body to be burned, but have not love, I gain nothing."

Then he went on to describe love and tell what it is and how it shows itself.

ABLE TO SPEAK MANY LANGUAGES — LOVE = 0

ABLE TO SPEAK LIKE ANGELS — LOVE = 0

ABLE TO PROPHESY — LOVE = 0

ABLE TO UNDERSTAND MYSTERIES — LOVE = 0

ABLE TO KNOW EVERYTHING — LOVE = 0

FAITH TO REMOVE MOUNTAINS — LOVE = 0

"Love is patient and kind," he said, "love is not jealous or boastful; it is not arrogant or rude.

"Love does not insist on its own way; it is not irritable or resentful; it does not rejoice at wrong, but rejoices in the right.

"Love bears all things, believes all things, hopes all things, endures all things.

"Love never ends; as for prophecy, it will pass away; as

for tongues, they will cease; as for knowledge, it will pass away. . . .

"So faith, hope, love abide, these three; but the greatest of these is love."

Then he added: "Make love your aim." And that is a very fine aim for you and me. We should seek to reveal the love of God in our lives at all times and in all places. At home, at school, at work, at play.

Not just silly sentiment, but love, true love. Love that is patient and kind. Love that keeps us from being jealous, or boastful, or proud, or rude. Love that never lets us insist on our own way or be irritable or resentful. Love that rejoices at good, but never at evil. Love that bears hardship without complaint, believes the best about others, is always full of hope, and endures suffering with a smile.

This is love at its best, said Paul. It is the kind of love that Christians should have in their hearts and reveal in their lives every day.

STORY 3

One Loving Family

PAUL carried in his heart a beautiful picture of what the church should be. He saw it as one loving family in Christ.

If there was one thing he couldn't stand, it was the suggestion that there could be divisions in the church, with Jewish Christians, Gentile Christians, and the like. Such an idea was quite wrong, he said. Those who accepted the gospel couldn't be separated. They all belonged together.

When the news reached him that the churches in Galatia were becoming divided over the question whether it was necessary to keep all the laws of Moses in order to be saved, he wrote them one of his strongest letters. "By works of the law shall no one be justified," he said. "In Christ Jesus you are all sons of God through faith. For as many of you as were baptized into Christ have put on Christ. There is neither Jew nor Greek, there is neither slave nor free, there is neither male nor female; for *you are all one in Christ Jesus*. And if you are Christ's, then you are Abraham's offspring, heirs according to the promise."

There was something far more important, he said, than trying to keep the letter of the law, and that was love. "For the whole law is fulfilled in one word, You shall love your neighbour as yourself."

Here he was back on his main theme again—love. It was love that mattered most to God. Love alone would bring peace and harmony into the church.

If they opened their hearts to the Holy Spirit, they wouldn't have to worry about breaking any laws. Love would keep them doing right. Love would stop them from biting and devouring one another in quarrels. They would stop doing everything unkind or hateful. For "the fruit of the Spirit is love," he said—"love, joy, peace, patience, kindness, goodness, faithfulness, gentleness, self-control; against such there is no law."

"If we live by the Spirit," he added, "let us also walk by the Spirit. Let us have no self-conceit, no provoking of one another, no envy of one another. . . . Bear one another's burdens, and so fulfil the law of Christ."

Whether the Galatian churches followed Paul's advice we do not know. But it was good advice, not only for them, but for us.

Here is the secret of unity, of getting on together, and it will work in church, or school, or home. It is as simple as A B C. It doesn't involve trying to keep a lot of rules and regulations, but merely saying earnestly to God, "Please fill my heart with Thy Holy Spirit." For God is love, and His Spirit is the Spirit of love. And when He comes in everything unlovely goes out.

This is the way—the only way—by which fathers and mothers, boys and girls, of all nations and tongues and peoples can become one loving family in Christ. It is the way to peace, friendliness, and happiness today, tomorrow, always. Why don't we follow it?

SELFISHNESS

DISOBEDIENCE

PRIDE

EVIL HABITS

STORY 4

God's Armor

WHEN Paul wrote from Rome to his old friends in Ephesus he reminded them that they too were part of the one loving family in Christ.

To those who had come into the church from pagan idolatry he said, "Remember that at one time you Gentiles" were "separated from Christ, alienated from the commonwealth of Israel, and strangers to the covenants of promise, having no hope and without God in the world. But now in Christ you who once were far off have been brought near in the blood of Christ. For he is our peace, *who has made us both one* and has broken down the dividing wall of hostility."

That is what the gospel does. It brings strangers together. It breaks down dividing walls.

"So then," Paul went on, "you are no longer strangers and sojourners, but you are fellow citizens with the saints and members of the household of God."

For this loving, united family he prayed a beautiful

135

GOD'S ARMOR

prayer, that they might go on learning more and more about God's love: "I bow my knees before the Father, from whom every family in heaven and on earth is named, that according to the riches of His glory He may grant you to be strengthened with might through His Spirit in the inner man, and that Christ may dwell in your hearts through faith; that you, being rooted and grounded in love, may have power to comprehend with all the saints what is the breadth and length and height and depth, and to *know the love of Christ* which surpasses knowledge, that you may be filled with all the fullness of God."

He begged them to "lead a life worthy of the calling" to which they had been called, "with all lowliness and meekness, with patience, forbearing one another in love, eager to maintain the unity of the Spirit in the bond of peace."

"Walk in love," he urged, "as Christ loved us and gave Himself up for us, a fragrant offering and sacrifice to God."

"Put on the whole armor of God," he said to them, "that you may be able to stand against the wiles of the devil."

Surely, he did not mean God wore armor like the Roman soldiers they saw every day. No, His armor is not made of anything material. Rather it is truth, righteousness, and love.

This is the armor every Christian must wear if he is to be victorious in all the battles of life.

"Stand therefore," said Paul, "having girded your loins with truth, and having put on the breastplate of righteousness, and having shod your feet with the equipment of the gospel of peace; above all taking the shield of faith, with which you

137

Wearing the helmet of salvation, the strong shield of faith, and the sharp sword of the Spirit, the Christian warrior is able to withstand all the fiery assaults of Satan.

can quench all the flaming darts of the evil one. And take the helmet of salvation, and the sword of the Spirit, which is the word of God."

Perhaps as Paul was writing these words he looked up at the tall Roman soldier standing beside him, admiring his brass helmet, his steel breastplate, his leather boots, his sharp sword, and gleaming shield. As he did so he thought of the humble Christians at Ephesus. He remembered the awful time in the theater there when for two hours the people shouted, "Great is Diana of the Ephesians."

"God's people could do with some armor like this Roman soldier is wearing," he thought. Yet, even more, they needed spiritual armor to help them resist all the temptations of the evil one and to keep their hearts pure, true, loyal, and full of hope and confidence in God.

Today many big department stores are selling armor again, specially for children. You can buy helmets, breastplates, and old-fashioned riding boots. You can even find swords and spears to complete the outfit and make you look just like one of King Arthur's Knights of the Round Table. But this isn't the armor we need most.

To live a good life, the life of love, the life of the true follower of Jesus, you need to wrap yourself in truth and put on the breastplate of righteousness, the shoes of peace, and the helmet of salvation. Then, with the shield of faith in one hand and the sword of the Spirit in the other, you will be able to face the worst of enemies unafraid. Clad in God's armor you are bound to win.

STORY 5

Eyes on the Prize

AS PAUL sat in his prison in Rome, and recalled all his many adventures while preaching the gospel, he thought with special tenderness of the Christians in Philippi.

There it was that he first saw the inside of a dungeon. He remembered the jailer who had washed his wounds and accepted Jesus the same night. There was Lydia, too, who had opened her home to him, and the other women with whom he had many times met for prayer on the riverbank. What wonderful people! How he loved them!

"I thank my God in all my remembrance of you," he told them in his letter, "always in every prayer of mine for you all making my prayer with joy, thankful for your partnership in the gospel from the first day until now."

"I hold you in my heart," he wrote. "For God is my witness, how I yearn for you all with the affection of Christ Jesus. And it is my prayer that your love may abound more and more

. . . so that you may approve what is excellent, and may be pure and blameless for the day of Christ."

As he wrote to the Galatians and the Ephesians, so now he had told the Philippians that he was most anxious that they remain united in the faith and "stand firm in one spirit, with one mind striving side by side for the faith of the gospel."

He urged them to be "of the same mind, having the same love. . . . Do nothing from selfishness or conceit," he said, "but in humility count others better than yourselves." "Do all things without grumbling or questioning, that you may be blameless and innocent, children of God without blemish in the midst of a crooked and perverse generation, among whom you shine as lights in the world."

That was a lovely picture he painted—with every member of the church, every man and woman, every boy and girl, letting his light shine, twinkling like a star on a dark night.

Then Paul went on to talk about himself and his hopes for the future. He had once held high office among the Jews. He had had money and possessions. "But whatever gain I had," he wrote, "I counted as loss for the sake of Christ. Indeed I count everything as loss because of the surpassing worth of knowing Christ Jesus my Lord. For His sake I have suffered the loss of all things, and count them as refuse, in order that I may gain Christ and be found in Him, not having a righteousness of my own, based on law, but . . . the righteousness from God that depends on faith; that I may know Him and the power of His resurrection, and may share His sufferings . . . that if possible I may attain the resurrection from the dead.

141

Paul was so devoted to Christ that he sacrificed wealth and worldly honor to become apostle to the Gentiles and a witness to the power and love of God and His saving grace.

"Not that I . . . am already perfect," he added; "but I press on to make it my own. . . . One thing I do, forgetting what lies behind and straining forward to what lies ahead, I press on toward the goal for the prize of the upward call of God in Christ Jesus."

He had his eyes on the prize that God has promised all who accept Jesus as their Saviour. He longed for the day of Christ's return, for the resurrection morning, and the joy of living forever with his beloved Lord. To him it was a prize worth everything it might cost in this life, and he wanted the Philippian believers to keep their eyes on it too.

"Therefore, my brethren, whom I love and long for, my joy and crown," he said, "stand firm thus in the Lord, my beloved. . . . Rejoice in the Lord always; again I will say, Rejoice. . . . Have no anxiety about anything, but in everything by prayer and supplication with thanksgiving let your requests be made known to God. And the peace of God, which passes all understanding, will keep your hearts and your minds in Christ Jesus."

Paul's epistle to the Philippians was perhaps his most tender and beautiful love letter. Because he loved these people so much he revealed to them the secret motives of his life, the glorious prize on which he kept his eyes.

It makes me wonder what prize is beckoning you. Is it money, or a big house, or lots of land, or an important job? Or, like Paul, do you reckon that nothing the world has to offer can be compared with the bliss of everlasting life with Jesus?

STORY 6

Love's Knitting

WHEN Paul began to write to the new Christians in Colossae he didn't get very far before he was back on the subject of love. To him nothing was more important than that the followers of Jesus should love one another.

First, he told them how pleased he was to hear of their faith and love; but he went on to say that he wanted them to become more loving still.

He was praying for them every day, he said, that they might "lead a life worthy of the Lord, fully pleasing to Him, bearing fruit in every good work and increasing in the knowledge of God."

It was his special desire, he added, that their hearts might be *"knit together in love."*

The original word has the thought of *bringing together*. Close together. As when one knots two pieces of string, or knits two pieces of wool, or welds two pieces of iron.

143

And that's exactly what love does. It brings people together. Fathers and mothers, parents and children, brothers and sisters, new friends and old.

And it does the best kind of knitting. People knit by love stay together—always.

Farther on in his letter to the Colossians, Paul came back to this same sweet thought.

He urged them to *put off* such unlovely things as "anger, wrath, malice, slander, and foul talk" and to *put on* "compassion, kindness, lowliness, meekness, and patience, forbearing one another and . . . forgiving each other." Then he added: "And above all these put on love, *which binds everything together in perfect harmony*. And let the peace of Christ rule in your hearts. . . . And whatever you do, in word or deed, do everything in the name of the Lord Jesus, giving thanks to God the Father through Him."

Here he was back to the knitting again—the knitting power of the love of Christ.

If things seem to be going to pieces around your home someday, if people are quarreling and saying unkind things to one another, you may be sure it is time for somebody to start knitting. Not with needles and a ball of wool, but with the tender, gracious, forgiving love of Jesus.

I hope you'll be the one to do it.

STORY 7

Comfort for the Sorrowful

P AUL had the same burden for the believers in Thessalonica as he had for all the others whom he had brought out of heathenism and Judaism into the Christian church. He wanted them to have more love for others. Unless and until their hearts were filled to overflowing with the love of God they would never be perfect Christians.

"May the Lord make you increase and abound in love to one another and to all men," he said to them, "so that He may establish your hearts unblamable in holiness before our God and Father, at the coming of our Lord Jesus with all His saints."

"You yourselves have been taught by God to love one another," he added; "and indeed you do love all the brethren throughout Macedonia. But we exhort you, brethren, *to do so more and more.*"

He wanted them never to be satisfied until the love that shone out of their hearts was a perfect reflection of the love of God in Christ Jesus.

But he had a special message for these dear people. Some of them were sad and discouraged because death had taken their loved ones. They were lonely, and puzzled, too, wondering why God had let their loved ones die.

Tenderly, kindly, Paul tried to comfort them.

"We would not have you ignorant, brethren, concerning those who are asleep," he wrote, "that you may not grieve as others do who have no hope."

Their loved ones were just sleeping, waiting for Jesus to come and wake them up.

"For," he went on, "since we believe that Jesus died and rose again, even so, through Jesus, God will bring with Him those who have fallen asleep."

He will bring them out of their graves just as Jesus came out of His grave.

PAINTING BY FRED COLLINS   BY REVIEW AND HERALD

"For this we declare to you by the word of the Lord," Paul continued, "that we who are alive, who are left until the coming of the Lord, shall not precede those who have fallen asleep."

In other words, one will not go ahead of another; we will all go home together.

"For the Lord himself will descend from heaven with a cry of command, with the archangel's call, and with the sound of the trumpet of God. And the dead in Christ will rise first; then we who are alive, who are left, shall be caught up together with them in the clouds to meet the Lord in the air; and so we shall always be with the Lord. Therefore comfort one another with these words."

There was no need for them to worry any more. No need to be sad. For Jesus was coming again, and He would give life to the dead on the glad resurrection morning. Then they would be "caught up together" to meet the Lord in the air.

"Together." That is God's plan. To bring loved ones and friends together again and to let them be together forever and ever. No more parting, no more sorrow, no more tears.

What precious words! "Together . . . always . . . with the Lord."

If you know a neighbor or a school friend who is sad and sorrowful, why not tell him about this blessed and beautiful hope?

STORY 8

Fight the Good Fight!

AS YOU may remember, when Paul was on his first missionary journey he came to a city called Lystra, where the people stoned him and left him for dead. There it was that he brought to Christ a young man named Timothy, together with his mother and grandmother.

At that time, or a little later, Paul asked Timothy to be his secretary and help in the work of spreading the gospel. Timothy agreed; and from then on there grew up a wonderful friendship between the two men. They traveled together, lodged together, and wrote together.

Paul loved Timothy deeply, looking upon him as his own son. When they were separated he sent the young man all sorts of good advice to help him in his work and keep him in the strait and narrow way.

Two of Paul's letters to Timothy still exist. You should read them. They are not very long. Their age—nineteen hundred years—makes them precious, but their greatest value lies in the good counsel they contain, given by an old man to a young man in the first century of the Christian Era.

"Train yourself in godliness," Paul wrote in his first letter; "for while bodily training is of some value, godliness is of value in every way, as it holds promise for the present life and also for the life to come."

"Let no one despise your youth," he said, "but set the believers an example in speech and conduct, in love, in faith, in purity."

To warn young people against thinking of money as the most important aim in life, he told Timothy that "those who desire to be rich fall into temptation, into a snare, into many senseless and hurtful desires that plunge men into ruin and destruction. For the love of money is the root of all evils. . . .

"But as for you, man of God, shun all this; aim at righteousness, godliness, faith, love, steadfastness, gentleness.

"Fight the good fight of the faith; take hold of the eternal life."

The second letter was written shortly before Paul was put to death in Rome. But though he was about to be beheaded, the apostle was more concerned about Timothy than himself.

"Shun youthful passions," he wrote, "and aim at righteousness, faith, love, and peace, along with those who call upon the Lord from a pure heart.

"Have nothing to do with stupid, senseless controversies; you know that they breed quarrels. And the Lord's servant must not be quarrelsome but kindly to every one, an apt teacher, forbearing, correcting his opponents with gentleness."

FIGHT THE GOOD FIGHT!

After reminding Timothy that his mother had taught him "the sacred writings" from his childhood, he said that these inspired scriptures, if read and studied, would make the man of God "complete, equipped for every good work."

Then he gave the young man this solemn charge:

"I charge you in the presence of God and of Christ Jesus who is to judge the living and the dead, and by His appearing and His kingdom: *preach the word,* be urgent in season and out of season, convince, rebuke, and exhort, be unfailing in patience and in teaching. . . .

"As for you, always be steady, endure suffering, do the work of an evangelist, fulfil your ministry."

Then he added this touching farewell:

"I am already on the point of being sacrificed; the time of my departure has come. *I have fought the good fight,* I have finished the race, I have kept the faith. Henceforth there is laid up for me the crown of righteousness, which the Lord, the righteous judge, will award to me on that Day, and not only to me, but also to all who have loved His appearing."

Paul had indeed "fought the good fight," and he wanted Timothy to fight it too. It was his earnest wish for every young man, every boy and girl, in the Christian church in those far-off days. If he were among us now, it would be his wish for you and me. To one and all he would say:

> "Fight the good fight with all thy might,
> Christ is thy strength, and Christ thy right;
> Lay hold on life, and it shall be
> Thy joy and crown eternally."

STORY 9

The Runaway Slave

IN YOUR Bible, right after Paul's two letters to Timothy, you will find two even shorter letters, one addressed to Titus, the other to Philemon.

The first of these contains much good advice to another young man who was helping to spread the gospel.

"Show yourself in all respects a model of good deeds," Paul wrote to him, "and in your teaching show integrity, gravity, and sound speech that cannot be censured."

Then he summed up the whole purpose of the Christian faith in these great words: "For the grace of God has appeared for the salvation of all men, training us to renounce irreligion and worldly passions, and to live sober, upright, and godly lives in this world, awaiting our blessed hope, the appearing of the glory of our great God and Savior Jesus Christ, who gave Himself for us to redeem us from all iniquity and to purify for Himself a people of His own who are zealous for good deeds."

Then, as now, the blessed hope of *the church* was the re-

152

Jesus said, "And I, if I be lifted up from the earth, will draw all men unto me," and countless millions from every walk of life have yielded to the appeal of His outstretched hands.

turn in glory of Jesus Christ. But the blessed hope *of God* was, and is, to gather out of the world "a people of His own," cleansed of "all iniquity," pure, holy, beautiful, and "zealous for good deeds."

As for Paul's little note to Philemon, while it's not very long, it is one of the most exciting books of the Bible. It is all about a runaway slave.

Philemon was the slaveowner and Onesimus the slave. Both had become Christians, but as yet Christianity had not done away with the old, hateful custom of slavery. It was still the law of the land that a Roman could buy any number of slaves he could afford. These poor slaves had no rights whatever. Often they were treated worse than animals. If they tried to escape, and were recaptured, their owners had the right to torture them or kill them as they pleased.

So when Paul brought Onesimus to Christ and learned that he was a runaway slave a delicate situation arose. Spiritually Onesimus was free, but legally he was still the slave of Philemon, whom Paul had also converted.

What to do? Should Paul tell Onesimus to go on trying to hide from his master, or send him back?

Paul decided to send him back and Onesimus agreed to go. And that's what this brief "love letter" is all about.

It is a model of tactfulness.

THE RUNAWAY SLAVE

Notice how graciously Paul approached the matter.

"I thank my God always when I remember you in my prayers, because I hear of your love and of the faith which you have toward the Lord Jesus and all the saints. . . . I have derived much joy and comfort from your love, my brother."

It was love that was needed just now. Lots of love.

So now, ever so gently, he came to the point.

"I appeal to you for my child, Onesimus, whose father I have become in my imprisonment. . . . I am sending him back to you, sending my very heart. I would have been glad to keep him . . . but I preferred to do nothing without your consent. . . .

"Perhaps this is why he was parted from you for a while, that you might have him back for ever, no longer as a slave but more than a slave, as a beloved brother. . . . So if you consider me your partner, receive him as you would receive me. If he has wronged you at all, or owes you anything, charge that to my account."

The Bible doesn't tell us what happened when Philemon received this beautiful letter. But the story has come down through the centuries that Onesimus was accepted as a brother and later became a leader in the church. Thus the love of God in Christ won one of its earliest victories over the wicked custom of slavery.

STORY 10

Keep Up Your Courage!

THE letter to the Hebrews was written to certain Jews who had accepted Christ as their Saviour. Paul sought to confirm the faith of these dear people and help them to keep up their courage.

"We must pay closer attention to what we have heard," he told them, "lest we drift away from it." "Take care, brethren," he warned, "lest there be in any of you an evil, unbelieving heart, leading you to fall away from the living God."

They needed to think more about Christ and His sufferings, and how He had been "crowned with glory and honor."

"Since," he wrote, "we have a great high priest who has passed through the heavens, Jesus, the Son of God, let us hold fast our confession.

"For we have not a high priest who is unable to sympathize with our weaknesses, but one who in every respect has been tempted as we are, yet without sinning.

"Let us then with confidence draw near to the throne of

157

Jesus often prayed to His Father in heaven in behalf of His disciples. How comforting it is to know that when we pray to God, Jesus intercedes in our behalf as our high priest.

ABEL

grace, that we may receive mercy and find grace to help in time of need."

Still worried about them, he urged, "Do not throw away your confidence, which has a great reward. For you have need of endurance. . . . For yet a little while, and the coming one shall come and shall not tarry."

To encourage them to hold on to the truth they had learned, he reminded them of the great heroes of the past who had stayed true to God no matter what the cost to themselves.

"By faith Abel" offered the right sacrifice, though it meant his death.

"By faith Enoch" walked with God in a very evil time.

"By faith Noah" built the ark when nobody had ever heard of rain.

"By faith Abraham" left his home not knowing where he was going. And "by faith Sarah" believed God when He said she would have a baby in her old age.

Again "by faith Abraham," required to offer his only son Isaac as a sacrifice, obeyed without question the strange

ENOCH

NOAH

SARAH

command, believing God could raise him from the dead.

"By faith Isaac" asked future blessings on Jacob and Esau.

"By faith Jacob" blessed the sons of Joseph.

"By faith" the parents of Moses hid him in the bulrushes.

"By faith Moses" chose to suffer hardships with the people of God rather than to enjoy "the fleeting pleasures of sin."

"By faith the people" of Israel crossed the Red Sea.

"By faith Rahab" gave shelter to the spies in Jericho.

It was a long list, but not long enough.

"What more shall I say?" asked the writer. "For time would fail me to tell of Gideon, Barak, Samson, Jephthah, of David and Samuel and the prophets—who through faith conquered kingdoms, enforced justice, received promises, stopped the mouths of lions, quenched raging fire, escaped the edge of the sword, won strength out of weakness, became mighty in war, put foreign armies to flight. . . .

"Some were tortured. . . . Others suffered mocking and scourging, and even chains and imprisonment.

"They were stoned, they were sawn in two, they were

MOSES

MOSES' MOTHER

ABRAHAM

JACOB

RAHAB

killed with the sword; they went about in skins of sheep and goats, destitute, afflicted, ill-treated—of whom the world was not worthy—wandering over deserts and mountains, and in dens and caves of the earth."

So he retold the moving story of the great heroes of faith. Then he pointed the lesson. With all these examples of loyalty, with "so great a cloud of witnesses" to think about, how dare anyone consider giving up the faith now?

Rather, he urged, let us "lay aside every weight, and sin which clings so closely, and let us run with perseverance the race that is set before us, looking to Jesus the pioneer and perfecter of our faith, who for the joy that was set before Him endured the cross, despising the shame, and is seated at the right hand of the throne of God."

Here is something for us to remember too. When we begin to feel discouraged we should try to think of others who have suffered for their faith far more than we have ever done. More important still, we should look to Jesus, who endured so much for us, and is now seated at God's right hand waiting to cheer us up.

Let us keep up our courage!

GIDEON

DAVID

STORY 11

God Is Love

THE last six books of the Bible—apart from the book of
Revelation—are really six short letters. Two of them
were written by Peter, three by John, and one by Christ's
own brother James.

Some think this James was later the leader of the church
council in Jerusalem, and his letter was full of good advice for
the whole church. He told the people to be glad when they
had trials, because trials would make them stronger Christians.
If they lacked wisdom, they were to ask God for it. They
were to be "quick to hear, slow to speak, slow to anger." And
they were to visit orphans and widows and keep themselves
"unstained from the world." This, he said, was pure religion.

But James's best advice was about the use of the tongue.
He must have run into a lot of trouble from careless gossipers.

Horses have bits to guide them, he said, even as ships have
rudders. "But no human being can tame the tongue." It can
set the world on fire, even as a small blaze can burn down a

forest. Only God can keep it under control. And for this He must give "wisdom from above," which is "first pure, then peaceable, gentle, open to reason, full of mercy."

"Do not speak evil against one another," "Do not grumble," "Do not swear," said James. And the wisdom of God would prevent all these faults.

Perhaps you and I need more heavenly wisdom to keep our tongues from saying the wrong words!

Peter's two letters are especially interesting because he actually lived with Jesus for three and a half years. The picture of a kind, loving, gentle Saviour, painted for us in the four Gospels, is confirmed by his writings.

"You were ransomed," wrote he, "not with perishable things such as silver or gold, but with the precious blood of Christ, like that of a lamb without blemish." "Put away all malice and all guile and insincerity and envy and all slander."

Jesus, said Peter, set us an example of patience and gentleness. "When He was reviled, He did not revile in return; when He suffered, He did not threaten."

162

GOD IS LOVE

So we should adorn ourselves "with the imperishable jewel of a gentle and quiet spirit, which in God's sight is very precious."

"Finally, all of you," he pleaded, "have unity of spirit, sympathy, love of the brethren, a tender heart and a humble mind."

Because he was sure Christ would return in glory to cleanse the earth with fire, he asked, "What sort of persons ought you to be in lives of holiness and godliness, waiting for and hastening the coming of the day of God?"

That is a good question for us to ask ourselves.

Turning now to John's three letters, we find that they breathe the same sweet spirit that won for him the name of "the beloved disciple," or the disciple of love.

In his first letter is to be found the test of a true Christian: "We know that we have passed from death into life, *because we love the brethren.*"

It is love that matters most to God—love shown by kind, friendly, compassionate deeds.

"Little children," wrote John, "let us not love in word or speech but in deed and in truth."

"Beloved," he went on, "let us love one another; for love is of God, and he who loves is born of God and knows God. He who does not love does not know God; for *God is love.*"

These three little words are the most wonderful in all the Holy Scriptures. Strangely, they do not appear until almost the very end of the Bible story. Yet in one form or another they have been there all the time—all the way from Genesis to John.

When Adam roamed the sinless earth he must often have whispered to himself, "God is love."

163

When the ark rested on Mount Ararat, Noah may well have said to his family, "God is love."

When Moses took the tables of the law from God's hands on Sinai, he almost said, "God is love."

When Israel entered the Promised Land their grateful songs said, "God is love."

When they returned from captivity in Babylon they cried again, in other words, "God is love."

When the prophets uttered their appeals and warnings they were really saying, "God is love."

When Jesus came to dwell among men He declared to everyone by word and deed that God is love.

And when He hung upon the cross of Calvary there was no longer any doubt that God is love.

The whole glorious plan of redemption is indeed summed up in these three simplest yet greatest words in the English language: God is love.

PART IV

Stories of Christ's Final Triumph

(REVELATION 1:1-22:21)

PART FOUR

STORY 1

The Voice Behind You

FOR the first fifty years after the crucifixion of Jesus the gospel of His love was carried far and wide by His faithful followers. Groups of Christians appeared in all the chief cities of the Roman Empire.

Farther and farther the message spread until it had been preached "to every creature under heaven." Alas, many people refused to accept Jesus as their Saviour. They didn't want Him to change their lives. They would not give up their evil habits. Angrily they turned against the Christians and hurt them in every way they could.

By the year A.D. 90 all the apostles save John had been put to death and he was an exile on the island of Patmos in the eastern Mediterranean.

Let us go back across the years and visit him there.

It is the Sabbath, "the Lord's day," and John is sitting on a rock, looking out across the wide blue sea. Not a bit like the young fisherman who once heard the call of Jesus by

167

In exile on Patmos, the beloved John was given a vision of the triumphs of the gospel message to that time when the New Jerusalem would come down from God out of heaven.

Galilee, he is now an old man with wrinkled face, gray hair, and long gray beard. Alone, cut off from all his friends, he is silently thinking of the past.

What memories crowd his mind! That first moment he met Jesus! Those kind, gentle eyes of the Master! His soft, loving voice! His earnest invitation, "Follow Me!"

He recalls the years of sweet companionship. What a wonderful friend Jesus had been! Truly the sweetest, noblest soul who ever lived. How tenderly He had ministered to the poor and needy! What joy and peace He had left in people's hearts wherever He went! It was hard to believe that some could have hated Him enough to crucify Him. Yet they had.

He remembers the trial of Jesus and the heartbreaking procession to Golgotha. The nails being driven through His hands and feet. His gracious words, "Father, forgive them; for they know not what they do." His kindness toward the repentant thief. His last thought for His mother. "Behold your mother!" He had said, and John had cared for her the best he could until her death.

He pictures the resurrection. What a day that was! Could he ever forget running to the tomb with Peter and finding it empty? Or that thrilling moment when Jesus appeared to the disciples, saying, "Peace be unto you"? Then it was that the glorious truth had dawned upon him that Jesus had indeed risen from the dead.

After that the Master had gone away to heaven. John can still see Him rising higher and higher, farther and farther, until "a cloud received Him out of their sight" (Acts 1:9,

168

THE VOICE BEHIND YOU

A.V.). He can still feel the loss and loneliness that came over him at that moment, and the upsurge of hope as the two men in white brought the comforting tidings: "This Jesus, who was taken up from you into heaven, will come in the same way as you saw Him go into heaven."

Sixty years had passed since then. And still the Master had not returned. Why? Could He have forgotten?

It is a pity He has stayed away so long, John says to himself. So many things have gone wrong. James has been killed. So has Peter—crucified upside down, some say. Paul has gone too, beheaded outside the walls of Rome. All twelve of the disciples are in their graves except John, and he is but one short step from his. Yet Jesus has not come back. There is no word, no sign from heaven. Nothing but silence. Sixty years of silence. Why? Why? Why? Can there have been a mistake?

Suddenly John hears "a loud voice like a trumpet." He looks around, startled.

And there, right behind him, he sees Jesus. There is no

doubt that it is He. Though His hair is "white as white wool, white as snow," His eyes "like a flame of fire," His feet "like burnished bronze," and His voice "like the sound of many waters" yet it is the same dear face he knows so well.

Overjoyed, John falls at his Master's feet. Gently Jesus puts His hand upon the old, bent head, saying, "Fear not, I am the first and the last, and the living one; I died, and behold I am alive for evermore, and I have the keys of Death and Hades."

It is as though He said, "John, you are not the last of those who founded My church. I am. And as long as I live My cause is not lost. Death may have taken Peter and James and all the rest. Death may take you. Never mind. I am alive for evermore. I have the keys of death. Someday I shall open the graves of all who believe in Me. I am Alpha and Omega, the first and the last. I was there at the beginning of the fight with evil. I shall be there at the end. The final victory will be mine. Hold fast your faith. I shall not fail you."

Should you ever feel downhearted, should you ever think you are the only one left who stands for right and truth, listen like John for the voice behind you. For Jesus is never far away, and His voice, like the voice of a trumpet, will give you courage to go on.

STORY 2

Conquerors for Christ

CHRIST did not appear on Patmos just to comfort His faithful old follower John. He had a message for His church, and He knew that John was the best one to pass it on.

"Write what you see in a book," He said, "and send it to the seven churches, to Ephesus and to Smyrna and to Pergamum and to Thyatira and to Sardis and to Philadelphia and to Laodicea."

These were the names of seven cities of those days in which the Christian faith had taken root. Each had its group of believers who were witnessing for Christ.

All of these groups, or churches, were dear to the Master. He pictured them as "candlesticks" or "lampstands" shining brightly amid the darkness of paganism. He was their Lord, walking continually among them, watching with deepest concern everything they did and everything that happened to them.

171

He was worried about some of them. Their lights were not as bright as they should be. Some members had lost their first love. Others were allowing worldliness to come into their hearts. So He sent them words of rebuke and warning, at the same time seeking to encourage them to do right, with promises of rich rewards for faithfulness.

To those who would overcome all evil and conquer all temptation He offered seven wonderful blessings.

172

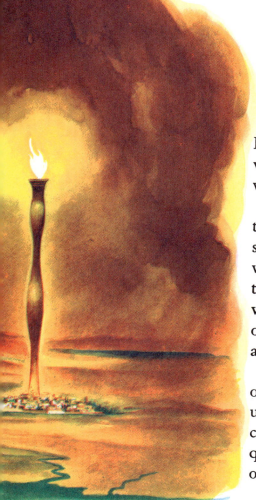

To the members in Ephesus He said, "To him who conquers I will grant to eat of the tree of life, which is in the paradise of God."

He wanted them to remember that, however much they might suffer for Him in this life, they would be amply repaid in the life to come. Paradise, beautiful Eden, would be their home, and the fruit of the tree of life their food, through all eternity.

To the persecuted Christians of Smyrna He said, "Be faithful unto death, and I will give you a crown of life. . . . He who conquers shall not be hurt by the second death."

Should they be killed because of their witness for Him, He would surely raise them up at the first resurrection, never to die again.

To the church in Pergamos He said, "To him who conquers I will give some of the hidden manna, and I will give him a white stone, with a new name written on the stone which no one knows except him who receives it."

In the holy of holies of the wilderness tabernacle there was a pot of manna, symbol of the spiritual food God provides

173

for His people. The faithful in Pergamos would have all of this food they needed. As for the white stone, this refers to a beautiful old custom. The giving of such a stone was a pledge of friendship and hospitality. So the Christian conqueror, or overcomer, may be certain of the eternal friendship and hospitality of Christ.

Thyatira was given this promise: "He who conquers and who keeps my works until the end, I will give him power over the nations; . . . and I will give him the morning star."

This assured the faithful that they would share Christ's final victory. If they suffered *for* Him, they would reign *with* Him. And they would possess the Morning Star, which is Christ Himself.

To Sardis He said, "He who conquers shall be clad thus in white garments, and I will not blot his name out of the book of life; I will confess his name before My Father and before His angels."

This was another glorious promise of future victory and eternal reward. Not only would the faithful ones have their names kept forever in the book of life, but Christ would personally tell the Father and the angels about their loyalty, ensuring for them a royal welcome into the courts of glory.

Conquerors in the Philadelphia church were told: "He who conquers, I will make him a pillar in the temple of My

God; never shall he go out of it, and I will write on him the name of My God, and the name of the city of My God, the New Jerusalem . . . , and My own new name."

This was a marvelous promise of everlasting fellowship with God. The conquering Christian will have God's name written upon him and also the name and address of his heavenly home. There will never be any doubt as to whom he belongs or where he belongs. He will be like a letter marked "Heaven—Special Delivery," and God will see that he gets there.

Lastly, the members in Laodicea were told: "He who conquers, I will grant him to sit with Me on My throne."

This was as if Christ had said, "The best of everything I have shall be yours." It meant that there was no limit to what He was willing to do for those who were true and faithful to Him. What more could He offer than that they should share His throne?

These wonderful promises were not, of course, only for the members of these seven churches in Asia Minor. They are for Christian conquerors everywhere, in every age. They are for grownups and children today. You too may be a conqueror for Christ. For He has offered not only the blessings of victory but the strength to be victorious.

Why not ask Him for this strength now?

STORY 3

Someone at the Door

"MOTHER! There's someone at the door!"

How often you have said this when you have heard a knock on your front door! And Mother has come hurrying out of the kitchen, patting her hair in place or drying her hands on a towel. Perhaps she has said to you, "Quickly now, put your toys away; tidy things up; it may be the minister."

Then the visitor has turned out to be the mailman, or a brush salesman, or the next-door neighbor come to borrow the lawn mower.

But though you may often be disappointed like this, a knock on the door is always exciting, for you never can tell who may have called to see you.

Suppose when you opened the door someday you would see Jesus standing there! That *would* be a surprise, wouldn't it? What would you do? What would you say?

It's not impossible, for in His message to the church in

176

SOMEONE AT THE DOOR

Laodicea, Jesus said, "Behold, I stand at the door and knock; if any one hears My voice and opens the door, I will come in to him and eat with him, and he with Me."

What a beautiful picture! Jesus standing outside the door! Gently knocking. Waiting to come in. Eager to come in. Listening for the click of the latch that will tell Him He is welcome.

Of course, He was thinking of the door of the heart. He wanted everybody in that church—rich and poor, old and young, parents and children—to know that He wanted to come and live with them, always. He longed to make every heart His home. But the promise wasn't only for them.

Jesus had said this very same thing to His disciples sixty years before, and John had written it down. "If a man loves Me, he will keep My word, and My Father will love him, and we will come to him and make our home with him."

How very beautiful! If *"a man"*—any man, any woman, any boy, any girl—is willing, God will make His home in his heart.

I know it doesn't seem possible, but it must be true, for

here Jesus says again, "Behold, I stand at the door and knock; if *any one* hears My voice and opens the door, I will come in."

That "any one" includes you.

He won't open the door Himself. He's too polite for that. Anyway, the latch is on the inside, and you have to lift it.

Maybe you can hear a knock just now.

There's Someone at the door! Someone very lovely, very kind, very dear.

Don't leave Him standing there! Don't keep Him waiting outside while you tidy things up. Fling wide the door in warmest welcome. Say, "Jesus, I'm so glad You've come. Please live in my heart forever!"

PAINTING BY RUSSELL HARLAN   ©   BY REVIEW AND HERALD

STORY 4

The Throne of God

JUST as John was thinking about Jesus standing at the door of his heart he chanced to look upward, and there was a door open into heaven.

"Come up," Jesus said to him, "and I will show you what must take place after this."

John didn't need a second invitation. He was eager to look into heaven and find out what was going to happen in the future.

So he peered through that open door and what wonderful things he saw!

In the center of all was the throne of God, a sight so glorious that he couldn't find words to describe it. A wondrous light shone from it, and all about it was "a rainbow that looked like an emerald." In front of it was "a sea of glass like crystal," while around it were twenty-four lesser thrones on which sat "twenty-four elders," clothed in white, and "with golden crowns upon their heads."

180

Then John noticed four strange creatures such as he had never seen before. One was like a lion, another like an ox, another like a man, and the fourth like an eagle, but they were all "full of eyes in front and behind" as if they were watching everything that was going on. And they never stopped singing "Holy, holy, holy, is the Lord God Almighty, who was and is and is to come!"

Now John's attention was drawn to the glorious Being on the throne, in whose right hand appeared a scroll with writing on it, and "sealed with seven seals."

"This must contain the story of the future that Jesus promised to tell me," he thought. And he was right. But first the scroll had to be opened.

Suddenly an angel called out in a loud voice, "Who is worthy to open the scroll and break its seals?"

There was no answer. It seemed as if the scroll must remain unopened. John wept, he was so disappointed.

Then a voice said to him, "Weep not; lo, the Lion of the tribe of Judah, the Root of David, has conquered, so that He can open the scroll and its seven seals."

John looked around for a lion and instead saw a Lamb "as though it had been slain." It was a symbol of Jesus, of course, and when He came forward to open the scroll, the twenty-four elders sang a new song, saying, "Worthy art Thou to take the scroll and to open its seals, for Thou wast slain and by Thy blood didst ransom men for God from every tribe and tongue and people and nation, and hast made them a kingdom and priests to our God, and they shall reign on earth."

Then John heard the most wonderful music he had ever heard. It came from a mighty host of angels, "myriads of myriads and thousands of thousands" of them. There were so many they seemed to fill all heaven, and they were singing heaven's hallelujah chorus, "Worthy is the Lamb who was slain, to receive power and wealth and wisdom and might and honor and glory and blessing!"

The majestic sound swelled louder and louder until it seemed as though every creature in heaven and on earth was joining in this glorious song of triumph, "To Him who sits upon the throne and to the Lamb be blessing and honor and glory and might for ever and ever!"

STORY 5

Horses of History

WHEN Jesus began to open the seals and unroll the scroll, it was just as if He had switched on a television set. One picture after another passed before John's eyes, each one a symbol of some event to happen in the future.

First he saw "a white horse, and its rider had a bow, and a crown was given to him, and he went out conquering and to conquer."

He recognized the rider. It was Jesus Himself. And the horse was His church, gloriously white in its first love and purity, as it went galloping with the gospel through all the Roman Empire.

As the second seal was opened "out came another horse, bright red" and its rider "was given a great sword" with which he took "peace from the earth."

John must have wondered whatever this could mean; and he was the more puzzled when, as the third seal was

184

opened, he saw "a black horse, and its rider had a balance in his hand."

But the fourth scene was stranger still, for now the horse had become a grayish color "and its rider's name was Death, and Hades followed him; and they were given power . . . to kill with sword and with famine and with pestilence and by wild beasts of the earth."

Whether Jesus explained these scenes to John we are not told, but looking back across the years, we can understand them clearly enough. The four horses were indeed horses of history. They pictured the story of the church of Christ for the next fifteen hundred years and more.

They showed how the church, once pure and beautiful, would lose its first love and become hardened and quarrelsome, seeking power from the state rather than from God. Then how it would forget that the gospel is free to all and would actually sell its blessings for money; and finally how it would become the very opposite of all that Jesus intended it to be. Instead of offering life, it would bring death to millions through its cruel persecutions.

It is hard to understand how Jesus could know that all these things would come to pass long before they happened!

But He did. History shows that His church was spoiled by sin just as He said it would be.

Had the moving pictures stopped at this point John might have thought that the preaching of the gospel would be a total failure and that Satan would win the long struggle between good and evil after all; but this was not to be.

When the fifth seal was opened John caught a glimpse of all the faithful followers of Jesus put to death because of their love and loyalty to Him, and he heard a voice tell them to "rest a little longer" till their number should be complete. God had not forgotten them. They would be rewarded very soon.

Then, when the sixth seal was opened, "I looked," says John, "and behold, there was a great earthquake; and the sun became black as sackcloth, the full moon became like blood, and the stars of the sky fell to the earth as the fig tree sheds its winter fruit when shaken by a gale; the sky vanished like a scroll that is rolled up, and every mountain and island was removed from its place.

"Then the kings of the earth and the great men and the generals and the rich and the strong, and every one, slave and free, hid in the caves and among the rocks of the mountains, calling to the mountains and rocks, 'Fall on us and hide us from the face of Him who is seated on the throne, and from the wrath of the Lamb; for the great day of their wrath has come, and who can stand before it?'"

What a tremendous scene! Without doubt it was shown to John to assure him that Christ would not fail to keep His

promise to return in glory and that, when He should do so, He would deal with all those who had treated His faithful ones so cruelly.

The "great earthquake" may well refer to the one that shook the world in 1755, as the fearful persecutions of the Dark Ages were coming to an end. The darkening of the sun and the bloodlike appearance of the moon took place on May 19, 1780, as we found when we studied Jesus' other prophecy about His second coming in Matthew 24 and Luke 21. The stars fell on the night of November 13, 1833, leaving only the final scenes in this picture yet to happen.

What about the seventh seal?

"When the Lamb opened the seventh seal, there was silence in heaven for about half an hour." Silence in heaven? How? Why? Because Jesus and "all His holy angels" will have come to this earth for His final triumph. On their return to heaven its courts will ring again with His praise.

If all these scenes should suddenly appear on your television set some evening, how would they affect you? If you should see the four horses galloping through history, picturing the sad, sad story of the church—what would you think? If you should see the promised signs of Christ's return, the great earthquake, the darkened sun, the blood-red moon, the falling stars, what would you say? And if you should see Him riding down the skies in all His glory, what would you do?

It's time to be thinking about these things, for surely, by now, He must be very near, "even at the doors" (Matthew 24:33, A.V.).

STORY 6

God Marks His Own

HAVE you ever divided a bag of candy among a group of friends? If so, as you passed the pieces around I suppose you said, "One for *you* and one for *you* and one for *you* and one for *me*." And then what did you do? I will guess that you picked up your pieces and put a mark on each so you would know yours from the others.

In the seventh chapter of the book of Revelation, John tells us that God is going to do some marking too. Just before Jesus returns in glory He will send a mighty angel all around the world to seal the servants of God in their foreheads.

Of course this doesn't mean that He is going to put a mark like a tattoo on anybody's head. That wouldn't mean a thing. Rather He will do something in the minds and hearts of men and women, boys and girls, that will be seen in the holy joy on their faces and in the goodness of their lives. By these everybody will know that they belong to God. And God will know it too.

189

As to how this sealing will be done nothing is said here, but Paul made it clear to the Ephesians when he said they were "sealed with that holy Spirit of promise" (Ephesians 1:13, A.V.). This is how God marks His own. Just as the Holy Spirit leads people to be born again so He brings them step by step into perfect oneness with Him.

Can anyone know when he is sealed? The only way to be sure is to give yourself entirely to God, praying for strength day by day to live in full obedience to His will. This means that you will ever try to live the pure, clean, beautiful life that you know He wants you to live. It means that you will seek to keep His commandments, all ten of them. It means that you will put no other gods above Him; you will never bow down to an idol of any kind; you will never take His name in vain; you will keep His true Sabbath as a holy day; you will honor your father and mother; you will never kill, or commit adultery, or steal, or lie, or covet your neighbor's goods.

In other words, you will love the Lord your God

with all your heart and mind and soul and strength, and your neighbor as yourself.

This means that your heart will be filled to overflowing with the love of God.

Thus, in the very last days of earth's history, when God searches among all nations for His remnant people, He will look for those who are so full of His love that they have become a perfect reflection of Himself. Not only do they "keep the commandments of God, and the faith of Jesus," but their lives have become beautified with love for God and men. To these God will say, "You are mine! And you, and you, and you!"

"They shall be mine," He says, "in that day when I make up my special treasure" (Malachi 3:17, A.V., margin).

Will you be among that happy company? Will you let God mark you as one of His own? Will you let Him seal you for His kingdom?

STORY 7

Last Message of Love

A S JESUS talked with John on the Isle of Patmos He spoke again and again about His second coming.

When He opened the seven seals it was to sketch the outline of events in His church until His Advent.

When He caused seven angels to blow their trumpets it was to reveal the story of the conquerors of the Roman Empire until He, the greatest Conqueror of all, should return and "the kingdom of this world" becomes "the kingdom of our Lord and of His Christ, and He shall reign for ever and ever."

When He told of the sending forth of seven angels with seven terrible plagues it was to warn the wicked of what will happen to them in the day of judgment.

And when He let John see the three flying angels it was to help him understand how hard God will try to save men before their last chance to return to Him shall have passed forever.

The first of the three angels that John saw "flying in

192

midheaven" bore "the everlasting gospel" (A.V.) to all who dwell on the earth, "to every nation and tribe and tongue and people." And he cried with a loud voice, "Fear God and give Him glory, for the hour of His judgment has come; and worship Him who made heaven and earth, the sea and the fountains of water."

The second angel cried, "Fallen, fallen is Babylon the great," while the third added this warning, "If any one worships the beast and its image, and receives a mark on his forehead or on his hand, he also shall drink the wine of God's wrath."

This threefold message is not really new. It is just the same old gospel of love God has been bringing to men since Adam first sinned in Eden. It is the *everlasting* gospel, changeless as God Himself.

It is an appeal to everyone in every country, every city, and every home, to turn back to God and worship Him as Creator and Redeemer before it is forever too late to repent.

It is a warning to flee from the follies and wickedness of "Babylon," to shun all the agencies of Satan such as "the beast and its image," and to avoid its mark like the plague.

10-13

For Satan marks his followers, too, just as God marks His. Only Satan's mark is the opposite of God's. It is seen in pride, greed, selfishness, and disobedience to His commandments.

As the three flying angels, their work completed, disappear into the blue of heaven, far in the distance John sees Someone on a white cloud "with a golden crown on His head, and a sharp sickle in His hand." As the cloud draws nearer and nearer he realizes that the One upon it is none other than Jesus Himself coming back in glory for His own.

This is why we know that the threefold message of the flying angels is due to the world just before Christ's second advent—why indeed, we know it is due to the world today.

Perhaps someday you will hear this message yourself. If you do, listen carefully and heed it well. It may be God's last message of love to you.

PAINTING BY FRED COLLINS

STORY 8

When Jesus Comes

HOW long John was allowed to look into heaven and see all the wonderful things Jesus wanted to show him we do not know. It may have been hours. It could have been several days and nights.

Any doubts he may have had about the return of Jesus were gone now. Any fears he had had that the pagan world would destroy the newborn church had vanished too. Had he not been shown the future victory of Jesus over all His enemies? Had he not beheld myriads of angels ranged on His side to bring it about?

Yet there is more for him to see—another scene of splendor and glory to sustain his faith in the final triumph of His Lord and Master.

Suddenly from the throne comes a voice saying, "Praise our God, all you His servants, you who fear Him, small and great."

In response, the whole vast multitude of heavenly beings,

like "the voice of many waters, and as the voice of mighty thunderings" cries out, "Alleluia: for the Lord God omnipotent reigneth. Let us be glad and rejoice, and give honour to Him: for the marriage of the Lamb is come" (A.V.).

The marriage of the Lamb! The wedding of Christ to His redeemed, the uniting of heaven and earth for all eternity!

Now John sees the Bridegroom coming for His bride. What a scene of glory it is!

"I saw heaven opened," he says, "and behold, a white horse! He who sat upon it is called Faithful and True, and in righteousness He judges and makes war. His eyes are like a flame of fire, and on His head are many diadems; and He has a name inscribed which no one knows but Himself. He is clad in a robe dipped in blood, and the name by which He

is called is The Word of
God. And the armies of heaven,
arrayed in fine linen, white and pure,
followed Him on white horses. From
His mouth issues a sharp sword with which to
smite the nations, and He will rule them with a rod
of iron; He will tread the wine press of the fury of the
wrath of God the Almighty. On His robe and on His thigh
He has a name inscribed, King of kings, and Lord of lords."

John watches spellbound as the sublime procession sweeps
in stately majesty down the skies.

WHEN JESUS COMES

Can this be the same gentle Jesus he once knew and loved in Galilee? he wonders. Can this be the One who meekly let Himself be crucified on Calvary's cross?

Yes, indeed, the very same. Unchanged with the changing years, but now crowned with the glory and honor He deserves.

And now a strange thing happens. "The beast and the kings of the earth" prepare to make war with the invading hosts of glory from above. It is a vain and foolish effort. They are swept aside, destroyed by "the brightness of His coming."

Does this mean that nobody will be glad to see Jesus when He comes again? Oh, no. It just tells what will happen to those who hate Him. His bride will be there waiting for Him—eagerly. His faithful followers will look up with joy saying, "Lo, this is our God; we have waited for Him, that He might save us. This is the Lord; we have waited for Him; let us be glad and rejoice in His salvation" (Isaiah 25:9).

In that day all who have died believing in Jesus will be raised from the dead and, with the living saints, be "caught up . . . to meet the Lord in the air" (1 Thessalonians 4:17).

And Jesus will smile upon them as a bridegroom smiles upon his bride, and He will take them home with Him to the "many mansions" He has prepared for them.

What a day of rejoicing that will be! Will you be glad to see Him too?

STORY 9

Good Wins at Last

NOW John looks far into the future. It seems to him that a thousand years go by. Then of a sudden he sees a beautiful city gliding down the skies, shimmering like a star.

Something about it reminds him of Jerusalem. But it isn't the old city he knew before the Romans sacked and burned it. No, indeed. It is a city more glorious than any he ever saw or dreamed about. Its foundations, walls, and rooftops are all aglow, shining like many colored jewels.

Gently it settles upon the earth. Within it are the people of God—those who were raised from the dead and those who were translated at Christ's second coming. They look radiantly happy after a thousand years in heaven.

Now John's attention is called to another amazing scene. Wherever he looks graves are opening and people are coming out of them. Millions upon millions. He has never seen so many. Yet they are all far different from the saints inside the city. Compared with them they look small and shriveled up. Their faces are hard and cruel.

Suddenly John understands. This must be the resurrection of the wicked Jesus told about long ago.

Now John sees a tall, powerful figure moving among the crowds. There is an evil look on his face, the look of one who knows he has been beaten and who wants to take revenge. It is Satan himself, the archenemy of Christ, who has caused all the trouble and sorrow on the earth since the beginning. Now he is spurring the wicked to attack the beautiful city.

"Its streets are made of gold, its gates of pearl," he cries. "Let us go up and take it. We are far more in number than those within it. Let's go! Let's go!"

Stirred with envy, greed, and hatred, the mighty mass moves forward, marching up "over the broad earth" and surrounding "the camp of the saints and the beloved city."

But that is as far as the wicked get. At that moment God steps in.

Says John: "I saw a great white throne . . . , And I saw the dead, great and small, standing before the throne, and books were opened. Also another book was opened, which is the book of life. And the dead were judged by what was written in the books, by what they had done."

It is the final judgment. And what a scene it is! Everybody who ever lived on the earth is present. All the good people are within the city and all the bad people outside it. In His wisdom God has brought everybody together at the same time so that all may understand what He has done and what He is going to do. He wants all of His creatures in His whole vast universe to know that His ways are right and good.

As the books of heaven are opened, not only do the wicked discover that God has kept a record of everything they ever said or did, but they see the whole story of sin from its beginning and what God did to meet it and overcome it. Maybe it will be shown on some sort of giant television screen, perhaps against the background of the sky itself.

They will see how sin began, and Satan's part in it. They will see how he brought the spirit of rebellion to this earth, with all its sad results. They will see Christ offering to pay the penalty of sin in order that the human race might not be destroyed. And they will see Him hanging on the cross, dying that men might live.

As the wicked look and listen they will realize that there was nothing more God could have done to help them. Some may even be sorry that they didn't heed the many calls to repentance He sent to them. Maybe Satan himself will be ready to admit his dreadful mistake. But it is too late now to repent. They should have done this long before when the chance was theirs.

At last, one by one, the books are closed. The record has been read. The story has been told. There is nothing more to say.

As John wonders what will happen next he sees a blaze of light sweep down from heaven as God mercifully brings the great struggle between good and evil to an end. And "fire came down from heaven and consumed them, and the devil who had deceived them was thrown into the lake of fire."

Thus, though it takes a long, long time, good wins at last.

STORY 10

All Things New

WHEN the smoke has cleared away and John is able to see around him again it seems that everything has changed. Everything.

The earth is different. The sky is different. And so much so that John says, "I saw a new heaven and a new earth; for the first heaven and the first earth had passed away."

Nothing marred by sin can be seen anywhere. Everything is gloriously beautiful. The whole earth looks as it must have appeared in the beginning when God created it. God has made it over again. He has restored Eden, just as He promised. He has made "all things new."

Deserts have disappeared. So have all the badlands and the great barren canyons left by the Flood. Gone too are all dead trees and scrawny bushes. All poisonous weeds and reptiles. All birds of prey. All fierce and cruel beasts. All disease germs. Nothing is left that ever brought harm or sorrow to man.

The same wonderful Being who once created the world with such infinite, painstaking care has now remade it with like skill and thoughtfulness for man's eternal enjoyment.

Everywhere John looks he sees beauty beyond compare. Towering mountains clothed with stately redwoods, hemlocks, cedars, pines, and oaks. Rolling hills adorned with flowering trees and shrubs. Grass-covered fields, dotted with masses of flowers like a vast, many-colored carpet. Buttercups and daisies, poppies and marigolds, bluebells and daffodils, hollyhocks and snapdragons, geraniums and delphiniums, orchids and begonias—all are here again as lovely as God first made them.

There is "no more sea." No more vast oceans separate people one from another. Instead are beautiful island-studded lakes, fed from one sparkling, rippling, cascading stream flowing forever from one central source within the Holy City. John says he saw this "river of the water of life, bright as crystal, flowing from the throne of God . . . through the middle of the street of the city." Thence it flows on to the ends of the earth, refreshing all nature with the life of God.

As for the New Jerusalem, it is so very beautiful that John can hardly find words to picture it. "Its radiance [is] like a most rare jewel," he says, "like a jasper, clear as crystal." It has "a great, high wall, with twelve gates." Yet it isn't like an old-world fortress, for the wall is of jasper and the gates of pearl, while the rest of the city is of "pure gold, clear as glass."

John specially mentions the foundations, for they are so very different. They are not made of concrete, or brick, or

206

heavy logs, but of all sorts of jewels. As the light from the throne shines through them they flash and sparkle in gorgeous colorings.

John looks for a temple, but there isn't one. There's no need for one any more. No more sacrifice for sin will ever be required, for Jesus made it "once for all." So "God and the Lamb" are the temple here.

"And the city has no need of sun or moon to shine upon it, for the glory of God is its light, and its lamp is the Lamb. . . . And its gates shall never be shut by day—and there shall be no night there."

What a wonderful home the dear Lord is preparing for

those who love Him! And what a happy one! For He is going to live with His people forever. With tenderest touch He will "wipe away every tear from their eyes" and nobody will ever be sad again. There will be no more death. No more sorrow. No more crying. No more pain. Only purest happiness forever and ever.

There will be no more grumbling. No more quarreling. No more fighting. Only perfect peace through all eternity.

There will be no more unkindness. No more impatience. No more cutting words or cruel deeds. Only loving friendliness always and always.

Would you like to live in this glorious homeland of God's true and faithful children? Would you like to be there when the saints go marching in?

You may. You are invited. "The Spirit and the Bride say 'Come.' And let him who hears say, 'Come.' And let him who is thirsty come."

"Come! Come! Come!"

Jesus is calling you. He wants you to share heaven with Him.

It is the last invitation in the Bible; the last in all the wonderful Bible story.

Why not accept it now?

INDEXES

Complete List of the 409 Stories

← PAINTING BY RUSSELL HARLAN   ©   BY REVIEW AND HERALD

Around every human life that trusts His love and obeys the principles of His kingdom the Heavenly Watcher puts His protective arms and keeps him from dangers seen and unseen.

COMPLETE LIST OF THE 409 STORIES

COMPLETE LIST OF THE 409 STORIES

Bible Men and Women

and Where Found in *The Bible Story*

BIBLE MEN AND WOMEN

INDEX THREE

Great Bible Teachings and Character-building Lessons

CHARACTER-BUILDING LESSONS

CHARACTER-BUILDING LESSONS

INDEX FOUR

Books of the Bible

and Where Mentioned in *The Bible Story*